THE CRAFTER CULTURE HANDBOOK

Published in Great Britain and the United States in 2007 by
MARION BOYARS PUBLISHERS LTD
24 Lacy Road London SW15 1NL

www.marionboyars.co.uk

Distributed in Australia and New Zealand by
Peribo Pty Ltd, 58 Beaumont Road, Kuring-gai, NSW 2080

Printed in 2007
10 9 8 7 6 5 4 3 2 1

A CIP catalogue record for this book is available from the British Library.
A CIP catalog record for this book is available from the Library of Congress.

ISBN 0-7145-3128-6   13 digit ISBN 978-0-7145-3128-1

Set in Georgia 11pt and Myriad 11pt
Printed by SNP Leefung, China

Mix It Up Cocktail Coasters from *Denyse Schmidt Quilts* © 2005 by Denyse Schmidt Designs
LLC. Used with permission of Chronicle Books LLC San Francisco www.chroniclebooks.com.

THE CRAFTER CULTURE HANDBOOK

BY AMY SPENCER

MARION BOYARS
London • New York

CONTENTS

Introduction

Needlecraft Revolution

Good As New

Electro Craft 101

Homemade Beauty 137

Home Sweet Home 159

Knitting in Public 201

- Red Light District Peekaboo Scarf – Shannon Okey (Knitgrrl)
- Super Chunky Tunisian Crochet Scarf – Tsia Carson (SuperNaturale)
- How to Knit a King Fish – Rachael Matthews (Cast Off)
- Fairytale Forest Hat – Zoë Ashton-Worsnop (Hello Mango)
- Body Count Mittens – Lisa Anne Auerbach (Steal This Sweater)
- Peace Knits Banner – Grant Neufeld (Revolutionary Knitting Circle)
- KoolAid Dye – Elizabeth Stottlemyer (Hobbledehoy)

Paper and Ink 251

- Take it to the Streets – Themba Lewis (Mt Pleasant Press)
- Go Gocco! – Kate Bingaman (Obsessive Consumption)
- Coptic Bound Sketchbook – Sugene Yang (All This Is Mine)
- Paper Pad Cozy – Jill Bliss (Blissen)
- Papier Maché Bangle – Rebecca Craig

Conversion Tables 282
Further Resources 283

Stuck? Please contact the individual crafters directly for help or advice with any of these projects. The publishers are unable to answer queries regarding the technicalities of the projects.

INTRODUCTION

The contemporary craft movement is a brand new phase in Do-It-Yourself culture, a practical and political reaction against consumerism. It is not simply about freedom of expression, but encourages us to think about the origins of the clothing that we wear, the products we use and the objects that fill our homes. 21st century crafters have adopted the movement as a form of radical social resistance. This isn't just some quirky trend for people who want to sew a new style of skirt or knit an unusual hat. These men and women are recycling carrier bags to crochet into shopping bags or building computer keyboards from old typewriters because they share a unified political stance. Concerned with the modes of production behind the average T-shirt available at ordinary retail outlets and fully aware of the exploitation a sweatshop labour force is subjected to, they believe craft provides an alternative to participating in an industry which is often unethical.

There is no all-encompassing 'Sweatshop Free' label that can help guide our purchases of clothing. Yet most consumers would prefer not to buy goods made in sweatshops or using child labour of the kind prevalent in South America, Eastern Europe, India and throughout Asia. At present China seems to be worst hit, with many global companies shifting their operations there because of favorable labour costs. Two-thirds of Chinese people are living on less than $1 a day and the average factory wage is just 40 US cents an hour – one-sixth that of Mexico and one-fortieth of the US (see the World Socialist website www.wsws.org). Think about that next time you wear a pair of cheap jeans for housework. The problem is that retailers are only just beginning to acknowledge a change in attitudes and the fact that people care – and this is where the craft movement comes in.

Anyone with creative impulses and a little time on their hands can get crafting. Feminists who previously shunned the joys of domesticity are learning that these forgotten skills are fun. Urbanites locked in isolated circles of work-focused living are enjoying the renewed sense of community. Others find the simple act of 'making something' a way to relax. DIY improvements around the home have always been popular, but why not take it one stage further? The projects in this book make an ideal starting place.

– Amy Spencer 2007

9

needlecraft revolution

In the 1980s, my mother belonged to a sewing group. A group of women met every week to sew little bags, purses and cushions to sell at the annual Sandy Bay Hospital Fair in Hong Kong. They went for the company, for relief from long days alone looking after small children and for the feeling that they were raising money for people less fortunate than themselves as well as for the sewing. They chatted and drank coffee and put together little fabric masterpieces by hand while keeping an eye on their children, those too young for school, playing under the big table on which they laid out their sewing. The older children joined them during the school holidays, impatiently rushing round the room, inventing noisy games to entertain themselves. On one of these hot, humid summer days, when I was five, I decided to join the adults round the table and learn to sew. I was allowed to use some of the fabric scraps to make something for myself. I had never sewn before but it looked simple. I picked a little square of pastel pink felt and another of white and was patiently taught how to sew them together. I sewed along three sides, attached a ribbon from one side to the other and decorated the front with sequins. I had made a handbag. It was too small to carry anything at all, it was falling apart and held together by some very large uneven stitches, but I was very proud of my little creation.

Some people will tell you that knitting is their thing, others that crochet is the only craft for them. I think that sewing is my perfect craft. By following patterns or making it up as you go along, you really can make anything.

Today most people in the West rely on buying everything. We pay for every little item, items that someone else has had to make for us. But people are increasingly turning to crafting what they need for their own lives. Some want to create their own unique clothing, making a genuine personal statement with what they are wearing. Some are concerned with creating exactly what they want to wear, if they can't find

clothing to suit their needs elsewhere. Others are actively protesting against globalization, taking a personal stand against the use of sweatshops in the garment industry.

Just as many people are returning to a self-sustainable lifestyle and growing their own food and harnessing solar and wind power, others are turning to craft. There appears to be a similar mood emerging to that of alternative cultures of the 1960s, when young people began to 'drop out' and embrace a more sustainable way of life. That this climate is repeating itself at the start of the 21st century is hardly surprising. In any period of social uncertainty there is a widespread feeling that people need to look after themselves.

The projects in this chapter are an introduction to this needlecraft revolution. They span a range of needlework techniques from simple hand stitching to creative embroidery techniques. Here you will find the basics as well as some more challenging ideas. All the projects here can be customized for your own needs. You can change anything, experiment, and play around with shapes, colors and textures. Take ideas and inspiration and then make something totally different. That is what I love about crafting. It can be as creative as you like. There may be some set techniques it is useful to learn but you can always experiment with them and create something unique.

Lara Newsom
HANDMADE PRETTIES

Lara Newsom started Handmade Pretties in 2002 as a way to make a little extra money. At first, she was making simple felt flower hair clips and lapel pins and selling them to friends and classmates at grad school. Eventually, she started selling to boutiques, and began experimenting with new shapes, materials and techniques. Currently, she makes brooches, hair accessories, purses, dolls, toys and more. She is always looking for new materials and techniques to keep her designs fresh and unexpected.

www.handmadepretties.com

'I was born crafty. Seriously, I was drawing, cutting, painting and gluing before I could speak in full sentences. I was very lucky to have come from a long line of creative people. One grandmother knitted and painted, the other did needlework and sewing. My father is a woodworker, and my mother was the girl-scout leader (and therefore the Queen of the hot glue gun). Wherever I went, there were craft supplies and people to teach me how to use them. By the time I was in college, I had adopted the motto "You can make that." Anything I wanted, I tried to make it first. I began amassing a huge craft book reference library, and though I have never had the desire to follow patterns, I often reference them to see how things go together when creating my own patterns. Previous generations of women fought hard for their place outside of the home. As goods became cheaper and wages went up, women no longer needed to make things for their homes, a trip to the local Wal-Mart covered all household needs. Or did it? Gone were the whimsical appliqués on jumpers, the doilies and embroidered tea towels, the crocheted French poodle toilet paper cozies, the Technicolor granny-square afghans, the patchwork whale-shaped pillows. Eventually, people realized that these things were handmade. Old-fashioned patterns were updated, grandmothers around the world found themselves holding weekly knitting lessons, and soon, skulls and crossbones were being knitted and embroidered onto everything. We are taking back our ability to shape the world around us. We are rediscovering our ability to make the things we were told we had to buy.'

Cookie Flower Pin

Lara Newsom

MATERIALS

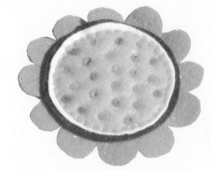

• Assorted color felt pieces
(wool/wool blend is best)
• Upholstery or button thread
• Needle
• 1" or larger bar pin
• Glue
• Scissors
• Hole punch

INSTRUCTIONS

Cutting Shapes

• Cut one felt circle that is 2" in diameter – this is the center circle.

• Cut one felt circle that is slightly larger than the first circle (so that about 1/8" is visible when they overlap).

• Cut two felt circles that are slightly larger than the second circle (so that about 1/8" is visible from under the second circle when they overlap). One of these will be the backing piece.

• Cut one felt circle that is about 4" in diameter. This circle will be cut into flower petals. Make twelve even cuts around the edge of the circle towards the center of the circle that are about ¾" into the circle. Carefully round all of the petal edges to form a circle with twelve petals around the outside.

• Using the hole punch, cut out small felt dots to be sewn to the center of the flower. Wool or wool blend felt works best with a hole punch. If you are having trouble using the hole punch, try sharpening it by using it to cut aluminium foil several times followed by waxed paper. It is also fine to cut the small dots with scissors.

Assembly

• Stack the felt circles on top of the petal piece, layering smallest to largest. Be sure to keep your back piece separate, it will be glued on after you have finished sewing. To keep the pieces from slipping while you sew, put a small dab of glue under each piece, be careful to keep the glue away from the edges.

• Using a needle and thread, start by tacking your thread to the back of the petal piece by sewing in place for several stitches. Starting from the back, poke up through all layers of felt along the edge of the center circle. Poke back through all layers except the center circle by placing the next stitch just outside of the center circle, but in line with the first stitch. Continue this with evenly spaced stitches all around the edge of the center circle. This is called an overhand stitch.

• Next, arrange felt dots across the face of the center circle. Use tiny dabs of glue to hold them in place, wait a few minutes to start sewing so that you do not knock off the dots. Sew up through all layers of felt from the back, including the felt dot, and then back down through all layers of felt including the felt dot (but not through the same hole). Do this until all dots are securely sewn down, and then tack your thread on the back of the flower by sewing in place several stitches (but not going through all layers of felt).

• Position the 1" bar pin in the center of the back of the flower. If there are holes on the bar pin, sew through these holes several times, making sure not to sew through all layers of felt. Using an overhand stitch, but only going through a few layers of felt, sew all the way down the body of the pin. Tack your thread and cut it.

• Position the backing circle on the back of the flower. Determine where the hinge and the clasp of the bar pin are, and cut a small hole so each can poke through the felt (the hole punch may come in handy for this). Apply a good amount of glue to the backing circle, and carefully position it over the pin, making sure that the hinge and clasp stick through the felt and are not covered in glue. Allow to dry overnight.

Vintage Fabric Felt Flower

Lara Newsom

MATERIALS

- Small square of vintage /print fabric (3½" x 3½" min)
- Assorted felts
- Upholstery thread
- Needle
- Scissors
- 1" bar pin
- Glue
- Hole punch

INSTRUCTIONS

Cutting Shapes

- Cut one circle that is 3" in diameter from the vintage/print fabric.

- Cut one felt circle ½" in diameter (this is the center of your flower head).

- Cut one felt circle that overlaps the center circle by about 1/8" all around.

- Cut one piece of felt that is about 3" x 3/8" (this is the stem).

- From the same color felt, cut one leaf shape that is about 2 ½" long by 1" wide.

- From contrasting colored felt, cut another leaf shape that is slightly smaller than the first leaf.

- From another contrasting colored felt, cut one leaf shape that is slightly smaller than the second leaf shape.

- Cut two rectangles that are 5" x 4".

The Flower Head

- Start by tacking your thread just inside the outside edge of the fabric circle.

Poke up through the fabric about 1/8" or closer to the edge of the circle. Poke down through the fabric about 1/8" from the first stitch in line along the edge, continue this running stitch until you have sewn all around the edge of the circle.

• Pull the thread tight to gather the edge of the fabric towards the center. Position the gathered center at the center of the fabric circle, and make sure the fabric is gathered evenly and looks visually pleasing. Poke the needle through the fabric to the back, and tack your thread. Position the two felt circles over the gathered center of the fabric flower. Poke your needle up through all layers of fabric and felt just inside the edge of the center circle. Poke your needle down through the outer circle and the fabric just outside the edge of the center circle. Continue with evenly spaced overhand stitches around the edge of the center circle.

• Tack the thread on the back, and set the newly created flower head aside.

The Leaf

• Stack the leaves from smallest to largest and tack them together using a small dab of tacky glue. Using a running stitch, sew just inside the edge of each smaller leaf.

• Once the smaller leaves are sewn down, poke the needle through all layers of felt at the base of the largest leaf. Place the needle down into the top layers of felt and then back up through the top layers of felt so that the needle is sticking in and out at the same time.

• Take the thread and wrap it around the tip of the needle and pull the needle through the fabric, stick the needle into the felt just barely below the first stitch you have just created and repeat the stitch, this is a chain stitch. Continue this stitch up the middle of the leaf to create the center rib.

• When you get to the last stitch, wrap the thread and pull the thread through, but then poke down through all layers just above the last stitch (this will hold the last chain in place). Tack the thread to the back and cut the thread.

Finishing

• Select one of the 5" x 4" rectangles and arrange the stem, flower head and leaf. When you have your arrangement the way you desire, tack each piece with a small dab of tacky glue.

• Using an overhand stitch, sew all around the edge of each piece.

• Trim the rectangle leaving a 1/8" border all around the flower.

• Position the bar pin along the stem of the flower and sew through the holes on the pin (if there are any) and use an overhand stitch to sew down the body of the pin, securing it without sewing through all layers of felt.

• Position the flower pin inside the second rectangle. Locate where the clasp and the hinge of the bar pin are and cut a small hole so they can stick through the felt backer.

• Cover the entire back of the flower pin with tacky glue, and carefully position the flower on the rectangle making sure the hinge and the clasp of the bar pin poke through the holes that you cut. Press down with your fingers and then allow to dry for several hours.

• Trim the back rectangle leaving a 1/8" border all around.

Abstract Blob Pin with Couching

Lara Newsom

MATERIALS

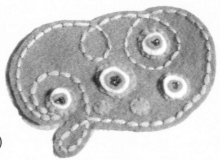

• Assorted felt pieces
• Assorted beads (seed and larger)
• Yarn
• Upholstery thread
• Needle (one for sewing one for beading)
• Bar pin (1 ½" or larger)
• Glue

INSTRUCTIONS

Couching (embroidery by sewing down yarn or string)

• First cut a rectangle approximately the size you want your pin to be. Using a fine marking pen (tailor's chalk is fine or even a Sharpie pen) draw an abstract shape with smooth curves that fills the rectangle. Make sure to leave some spaces that are large and others that are small (the large spaces will later be filled in with circles of felt and beadwork).

• Pick a starting point for the couching, and tack down the yarn to the felt by sewing in place for several stitches. Lay the yarn down on top of the line you drew.

• Stick the needle into the felt on one side of the yarn and poke it out on the other side just a little diagonal from the first stitch.

• Pull the thread tight.

• Poke the yarn through the felt along the edge of the yarn on the first side again be sure to position the stitch directly across the yarn from the second stitch and poke through to the other side of the yarn diagonally again. Doing your stitch this way will create stitching that is straight across the yarn.

• Sew down the yarn to cover the abstract line you drew.

• When you reach the end, poke the thread to the back and tack it.

• Trim around the edge of your blob leaving about 1/8" all around.

Circles

• Cut several small circles from the assorted felts. Make the pieces so that they will fit inside the spaces you left inside the abstract blob. Try several different layouts until you find something that is pleasing, and then tack down the circles using tiny dabs of tacky glue.

• Using an overhand stitch, sew around the edges of the circles.

Beads

• After you have sewn down all of the circles, decide if you would like to add bead clusters to the pin. I like to add small clusters of seed beads inside the circles, but sometimes like to add a single larger bead inside the circles or on its own. Using your beading needle and a finer thread, sew down the beads. First tack the thread to the back of the pin, and then poke up through all layers where you would like to put the bead.

• Place the bead on the needle and push it down onto the thread. Poke the needle down through all layers of felt and tack the thread. Do this until all beads are sewn down.

• Tack the thread and cut it.

Finishing

• Place the bar pin on the center of the back of the blob pin. Using the regular needle and upholstery thread, sew the bar pin to the back. If there are holes on the bar pin, be sure to sew through the holes several times.

• Then, using an overhand stitch, sew down the body of the bar pin.

• Cut a rectangle that is bigger than the blob pin. Place the rectangle over the back of the blob pin and cut holes where the clasp and hinge of the bar pin will poke through.

• Cover the back of the blob pin with tacky glue, and then position the backing rectangle over the pin being certain that the hinge and the clasp of the bar pin poke through the holes that you cut.

• Allow to dry for several hours, and then trim around the edge leaving a 1/8" border all around.

Laural Raine
THIMBLE

Laural Raine has been keeping a blog about her projects – successes and failures – for almost two years, and runs Thimble, a small online shop selling her handmade knitting and craft cases, purses, buttons and accessories.

www.thimble.ca

'I get a lot of my crafting inclinations from my mother, who taught me to knit and sew and bake when I was quite young. However, I got my first sewing machine that was really my own for my twentieth birthday, and really started crafting a lot after that, learning to quilt and eventually starting my website and beginning to sell some of the things I was making. Now as an adult I think crafting is so important to my life as a creative outlet that is separate from my job and anything else I might be doing. It feels really great to have something to do with my spare time that is productive and challenging, where I can constantly see my skills growing and challenge myself to learn new things.

There are many people who grew up like me, with mothers who had been taught all these craft skills by their mothers when they were young and then were still practising those skills with their children – in part because of the values of the counterculture of the 1960s and 1970s. So many of us had those skills lying dormant for a few years, after rejecting everything that our parents taught us as teenagers. We've come back to it, in part because of social and political ideas about the environment and socially just labour practices. An interest in craft has just resurfaced again as part of a wider movement to find something unique and creative in a world of otherwise mass-produced products; to have some kind of creative hobby so that your main form of entertainment isn't just going to the mall on the weekend.'

Crafty Tool Pack

Laural Raine

MATERIALS

- Two pieces of fabric 22" x 11" (A)
- One piece of fabric 21" x 11" (B)
- One piece of fabric 22" x 7 ½" (C)
- One piece of fabric 22" x 5 ½" (D)
- 32" length of ribbon
- One button

INSTRUCTIONS

- Begin with fabric C. Create a hem by folding the long edge over 1/4" and press. Then fold it over again 1/4". Press and stitch along the entire edge to create a 1/4" hem.

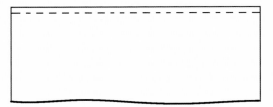

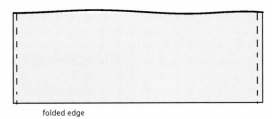

folded edge

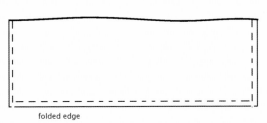

folded edge

- Repeat with fabric D.

- To create the flap, take fabric B and fold it in half the long way, with right sides together. Sew a 1/4" seam down both of the short sides.

- Turn right side out, pushing the fabric out flat at the corners. Press flat with an iron. Top stitch around the three closed sides, 1/4" from the edge.

- Lay out one piece of fabric A, right side up. Place fabric C on top, then place fabric D on top of this, lining up the bottom edges of all three pieces. Pin together.

- To create pockets, stitch through all three layers. Depending on what you want to store in your crafty tool case, you may want to vary the size of the pockets. To make the case as pictured, stitch lines at the following intervals: 7 1/4",

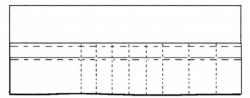

8 3/4", 10 1/4", 11 3/4", 13 1/4", 14 3/4", 16 3/4", 18 3/4". You may want to use tailor's chalk or a quilting marking pen to measure and draw your lines before stitching them.

Assembling the Case

• Lay out the piece with the pockets right side up. Lay the flap on top of this, with the unfinished edge aligned with the top edge of the pocket piece. Double the piece of ribbon in half, and lay on top of the pocket piece with the end aligned with the left edge of the pockets.

• Lay second piece of fabric A on top of everything, right side down. Pin all layers

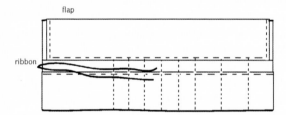

together, then stitch through all layers around all four sides, leaving a 3" gap along the right side.

• Turn the whole thing right side out through this 3". Press flat. Slip stitch the 3" opening shut. Top stitch 1/4" from the edge around all four sides, and on the top edge, topstitch over the flap as well.

• The case should now fold into thirds. Sew the button onto the exterior of the middle section so it aligns with the ribbon.

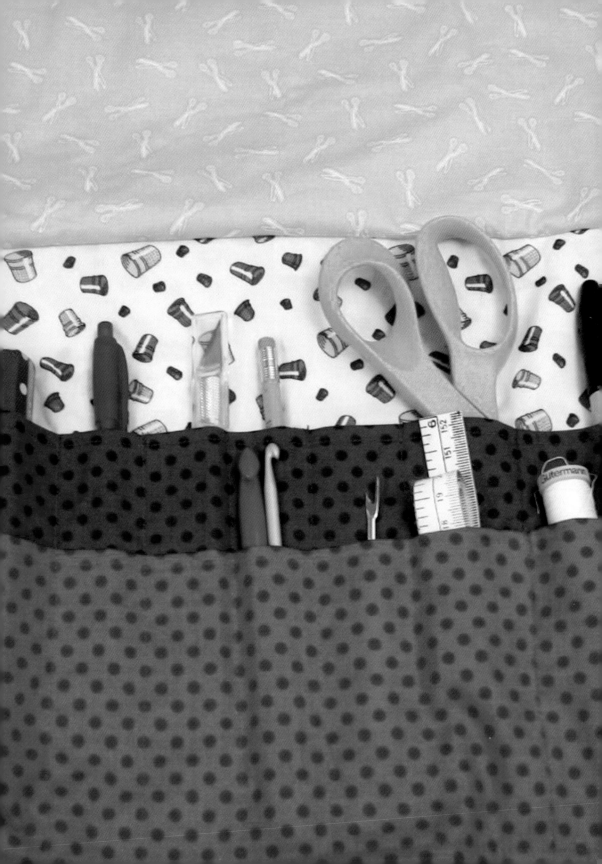

Heather Treadway
PAPER DOLL FASHIONS

Heather Treadway is certainly my kind of crafter. She imagines what she wants and then just makes it – no fuss, no trouble. A childhood love of fashion has spawned her own clothing label, Paper Doll Fashions, and the results are one-of-a-kind pieces with a playful edge.

www.paperdollfashion.com

'In 2001 I sold my first skirt to a local shop. The skirt was made out of a pillowcase, was not cut with any attention to which way the grain of the fabric was going, had a drawstring for a closure, and was certainly not lined. It sold. I made more items until I reached out to other stores in Seattle and created my own name – Paper Doll. I thought it described my style, cut from one piece of fabric, plain colors, simple, not sexy, flat.

I started selling on www.buyolympia.com, and in other stores around the US. In 2003 I really felt like everything I did or bought or created affected or had the potential to affect Paper Doll. I still don't make much money, but right now that doesn't matter very much. In 2004, my friends and I opened a non-profit clothing collective called the Olympia Clothing Project. At any given time we would have up to twenty different designers selling their wares. They were given one hundred percent of the cost of the item. We also held art shows and parties in that space and I highly recommend putting together something like that, as people are becoming increasingly supportive of community-run, non-profit, independent, locally made, craft and fashion shops and galleries. People who are consciously aware of the production of their goods are seeking more ethical and personal businesses and individuals to support. Have you ever knitted a sweater? It takes so long. You're really involved in its making. You're part of that sweater, and the memory of making it becomes a part of you.'

Laptop Case

Heather Treadway

You may have a trustworthy laptop that you can't bear to be parted from – it seems such a shame to carry it around in those ugly, plain covers that you see for sale. There doesn't seem to be much choice. That's exactly where the idea of making-it-yourself comes in. This project is for a one-of-a-kind, super handy, soft and cuddly laptop case. You can make your own decisions and design the whole thing for yourself. Think creatively and anything can happen.

MATERIALS

• One piece of medium weight fabric (corduroy, cotton twill, or sweatshirt fleece) for outside of case (A)
• One piece of lighter weight fabric (thin lightweight cotton) for lining of case (B)
*Fabric should be at least 45" x 15"
• 5" x 7" piece(s) of fabric for pocket (C)
• 6" of velcro or three velcro dots
• Scissors
• Ruler
• Pen
• Sewing machine
• Iron

INSTRUCTIONS

Find Your Materials

• Chose the fabric you would like to create your case. You will need two different kinds of fabric, one for the outside and one for the lining. If you want you can take a large sweatshirt or corduroy jacket to cut up, and for the lining you can use a sheet, old pillow case or T-shirt. Whatever you choose should be pre-washed and pretty big. The pocket of the laptop case can be made out of any scrap of fabric you choose, the final dimensions being 4" x 6".

Measure and Cut

• Lay out piece A right side facing down, on a large flat surface. Using your ruler and pen measure and draw a rectangle according to the size of your lap top:

For 12" iBook – 30 x 11.5
For 15" iBook – 36 x 12
For 17" iBook – 40 x 12

• Now lay piece B right side down on the table and use the same measurements as the outside of the case and cut an identical rectangle.

Make the Pocket

• It's time to cut out your pocket. This is the fun part because the pocket is small, so there is a lot of room for creativity. I sewed a patch of my friend's band on the front of my pocket, you can get crazy and paint on a piece of fabric, or sew many pieces of fabric together to make a quilted-looking pocket, or just use the same fabric you used for the case. If you decorate your pocket, make sure to do it before you sew it to the case. If the fabric is thin, you'll want to cut two pieces. If durable, you'll only need one. Cut your rectangular pocket 5" x 7". You'll need to cut two rectangles this size if the fabric is really thin.

You now have all of your pieces cut and are ready to construct. If your pocket is made from two pieces of thin material:

• Take one of the 5" x 7" pieces and find the right side of the fabric.

• Fold down one of the 5" sides (the top of the pocket) about ½" and press with the iron, making sure the folded flap is pressing against the wrong side of the fabric.

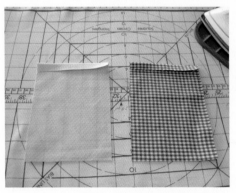

• Do the same with the other rectangular pocket piece.

• Now, take your pieces over to the sewing machine and pin them together (right sides together, flaps out).

• Sew along the two sides and bottom of the pocket.

• Turn inside out, and sew the tops together. The flaps should be INSIDE the pocket. Don't give much of a seam allowance, as close to the top as possible is nice.

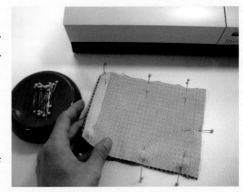

If your pocket is made from one piece:

• Fold down one of the 5" sides, the top of the pocket, about 1/4" and press with the iron, fold another 1/4" and press with iron again. Make sure you've folded the edge so the right side of the fabric is flat and the wrong side is touching the hemmed edge.

• Fold the sides and bottom in about ½" and press with the iron. The finished pocket should have hemmed and pressed clean edges.

• Sew across the top edge of the pocket to hold down that top hem.

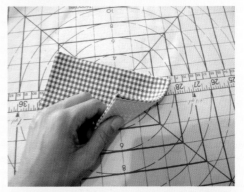

Attach Pocket to Case

• Take piece A and fold length ways so the bottom half of fabric is about 4" longer than the top half, lay the pocket over the lower left quarter of this smaller rectangle leaving about 1.5" space between the bottom and left edge of case, this is where you will attach your pocket. Open piece A, leaving the pocket there and pin the pocket to the fabric.

• Sew along the two sides and bottom of pocket

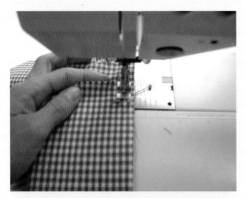

Sew Side Seams

• Take piece A and fold as you did to find the placement of the pocket, one side being about 4" shorter than the other, with the pocket on the shorter side, facing the fabric right sides together (pocket will be inside).

• Pin and sew along edges with a 5/8" seam-allowance from bottom of bag to 5/8" from the top of the bag.

• Now do the same for piece B. Fold so the bottom half is 4" longer than the top half of fabric, pin and sew the sides together, following the seam up to ½" before the top of the case.

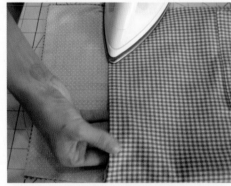

Sewing the Top Edges of Case

• Turn the outer case right sides out, and put the inner case inside the outer case making sure the inner case has the right side facing inwards.

• Take your case to the ironing board.

• Align the inner bag neatly into the outer bag matching the side seams to each other. You have 5/8" of space at the top of your side seams so you can fold the top edges of your inner and outer cases into each other, fold down 5/8" along entire length of the edges of your bags, following the shape. Press firmly with iron and pin together, you are connecting the inner and outer bags and folding in the edges so they are clean.

• Starting at the corner of the lower edge using a 1/4" or less seam-allowance sew along bottom edge of opening, then take a sharp turn and follow up the soon to be flap of your case and back down to meet your seam.

Sewing on the Velcro

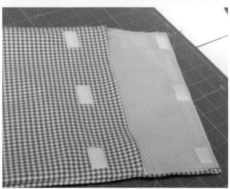

• Lay the three pieces of the hook side of the velcro along the top inner flap of the case. Make sure that they are set evenly apart and pin securely.

• Fold flap over the case and mark where the partner velcro pieces must go, or you can gently attach the soft pieces to the hook pieces and lay the flap over, then carefully pull off the soft pieces and pin to their correct placements.

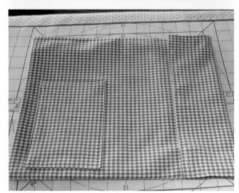

• Sew around all edges of velcro piece. Repeat for other velcro pieces.

Craft Fairs

Along with this new wave of crafting has come a new form of craft fair, places for crafters to sell their wares

THE RENEGADE CRAFT FAIR

www.renegadecraft.com

The Renegade Craft Fair is a DIY event started by Sue Blatt and Kathleen Hubbley in 2003. The pair wanted to sell what they made at local fairs, which seemed simple enough but they soon realized that there wasn't a fair suitable for their crafts. They decided to organize their own.

BAZAAR BIZARRE

www.bazaarbizarre.org

Bazaar Bizarre began in 2001 in the Boston-area, as a hotch-potch of friends and acquaintances cobbling together their handcrafted DIY wares to sell and staging an offbeat entertainment extravaganza. The event has now spread to Cleveland, Los Angeles and San Francisco.

CRAFTIN' OUTLAWS

www.craftinoutlaws.com

Craftin' Outlaws is an annual alternative craft fair held in Columbus, Ohio. Its aim is to counter the homogenized shopping experience in their town and showcase indie crafters.

NO COAST CRAFT-O-RAMA

www.nocoastcraft.com

The No Coast Craft-o-Rama is a craft event that began in 2005 in Minneapolis as a way to feature a variety of designers, artists, crafters and other talented creators of unique handmade goods.

URBAN CRAFT UPRISING

www.urbancraftuprising.com

In the spring of 2005, five indie crafters banded together to organize the largest alternative, urban craft fair the Northwest had ever seen. Urban Craft Uprising was born. The group dedicated itself to creating a unique showcase for rising indie craft stars and to provide the people of Seattle with the chance to shop for one-of-a-kind creations.

Vanessa Brady
GERBERA DESIGNS

Vanessa Brady began sewing handbags after not being able to find a purse that fit her personality. After a year of having friends and strangers ask where she bought her eclectic bags, Gerbera Designs opened its online doors. Now Vanessa continues to design and sell unique iPod covers, bags and other fun accessories through her online shop as well as in a number of retail shops throughout the world.

www.gerberadesigns.com

'I sat in front of a borrowed sewing machine late one night in 2003. I had only the most basic of sewing skills – the sewing machine was still a foreign entity to me – but hopefully enough stubbornness and determination to see the project through.

The road to creativity began when I was a child and my mother insisted that I do more than watch TV. Never one for boredom, she had an unlimited supply of craft projects for my sisters and I to try. In fact, I still have the first pillow my mother taught me the basics of sewing with. There really isn't much to it but it was a good start at ten years old. After a small hiatus of about fifteen years where the young (and naive) feminist in me, decided that real women don't sew, I once again found myself wanting to follow in the footsteps of my mother and her mother before her. Unable to find a bright red messenger bag, I decided to take matters into my own hands.

Fast forward eight hours, three spools and countless number of ripped seams and curses, I was finally the proud owner of my first red messenger bag. Never mind that I couldn't really put anything in my new bag because the bottom would fall out or that all the seams were already unravelling since I didn't know about fraying or linings. I was proud to say, I had made a bag with my own two hands and that has made all the difference.'

Vinyl Sneaker Pouch

Vanessa Brady

Pouches are always fun to sew. They have all the personality of a purse with half the effort. If you don't already, you're going to love working with vinyl. It's thick and durable…and no animals were harmed for the sake of fashion.

MATERIALS

- Two pieces of vinyl 9.5" x 6.5"
- Two pieces of fabric (lining) 9.5" x 6.5"
- One piece of white fabric 9" x 6"
- Zipper
- X-acto knife
- Sewing materials
- Stencil (for the heart shape on the sneaker)

INSTRUCTIONS

Basic Pouch Tutorial

- Place front of pouch on table. Layer zipper and lining on top of front, right sides facing each other. You want the teeth of the zipper pointing downwards.

- Sew along the edge. If you're lazy (like me!), you hate switching to your zipper foot so I just move my needle alignment to the far left and use the zipper teeth to guide my foot. Repeat steps 1 and 2 for other side of pouch.

- Flip layers so that the wrong sides of the fabrics are facing. Press the zipper seam with an iron.

- Using the teeth once again as a guide, secure seam with your sewing machine.

- Unless your zipper is exactly the right size, you're going to have to shorten it. Luckily for you, it's very easy to do! Just cut off the excess amount and sew (using a zigzag stitch) the barrier. This will prevent the zipper from falling off.

• Flip your fabric again, so that the right sides of each of the fabrics are facing.

• Making sure your edges are aligned, measure and cut 1" squares in each of the corners.

• Beginning bottom middle of your lining, begin to sew around the entire outside of pouch. Give yourself about a 3" gap at the base of the lining so that you can flip your pouch right side out. Don't forget to open the zipper before you begin sewing!

• Pinch edges together and sew across. Make sure that your seams are flat against each other in opposite directions.

• Reach inside the lining gap to pull the outside fabric through and out. Take your time, you don't want to rip your lining this close to being done! Sew lining closed and push inside the pouch.

• *Tada!* You now have your own handy dandy, oh-so-cute pouch!

Sneaker Design

• Photocopy the sneaker stencil (left).

• Using an X-acto knife (or similar) carefully cut out all the black parts of the stencil. Don't forget to save the cut out bar from the shoe's sole and your heart.

• Trace and cut your stencil onto the vinyl.

• Using tape to secure it, position your white fabric to the back of the vinyl. Make sure the fabric is somewhat tight. You don't want the fabric to pull and crease when you begin sewing.

• Front side up, begin sewing around all the openings. Try to get as close to the edge as possible. This is quite tedious (especially around the shoe laces!) but you'll like the end result. Trim away the excess white fabric.

• Position and sew black stripe on sole and heart in circle.

Emerald Mosley
GOLDTOP

Emerald Mosley is a London based self-employed interactive designer, who also finds time to perform with all-girl dance troupe The Actionettes. She uses her website as a place to share her crafting experiences and ideas for new projects, as well as writing a blog about her increasingly creative life.

www.goldtop.org

'I have always made stuff, ever since I was little. I learnt from family and school and it just carried on. I made a robot that had flashing eyes with my mother, conker furniture for dolls with my grandmother, how to cook with my father, how to knit with my other grandmother and I sewed my first needle book from felt at primary school.

It's fun. It's great being able to make something and have it there, in real life. You can make things that are unique, not something mass-produced. It's a satisfying feeling.

I like to keep on learning new stuff and it's a challenge to figure out how things are made. Recently I've been knitting, sewing, making my first dress, sawing wood, growing tomatoes, baking and am now interested in dyeing my own yarn and trying crewel embroidery.

It's okay to do craft again – it's more inclusive, and no longer the domain of children or grandmothers. It feels like a post-feminist thing too, you're not thinking about it being too "girly" any more – you just get on with it. It's fun to be part of the Do-It-Yourself ethic – why pay £60 for a skirt you could easily make yourself? Why have the same as everyone else?'

Little Birds Mobile

Emerald Mosley

Emerald Mosley has a mysterious ability for making the cutest things imaginable. This project is fantastic for introducing you to many different skills, as well as teaching you some new embroidery stitches and encouraging you to think about how you can use them to decorate fabric. Felt is one of the most versatile and sturdy fabrics and comes in such wonderful colors you really can use it for so many different uses anything your imagination can conjure up. You can reuse the techniques and ideas to create your own plush toys.

MATERIALS

- Felt (wool if possible; it's thicker, cuts cleaner and feels nicer) – various colours
- Sewing thread, embroidery thread – various colours
- Acrylic or fabric paints – various colours
- A 25cm length of thin doweling or bamboo
- Nylon thread – enough to hang branch the height you want!
- Toy stuffing (Kapok or similar)
- Toy beads (you can use dried beans or rice as weight instead)
- Some sewing needles, three safety pins

INSTRUCTIONS

- First photocopy the templates on page 43, scaling the images up to fit on an A4 sheet of paper.

- Lay all templates on felt, A sides up (where applicable).

- Draw around them, and then cut out.

- Now flip over branch, small bird, small bird wing, large bird and large bird wing, B-side up and draw around them again and cut out. This will ensure any drawing lines will be hidden when you place pieces together!

• Draw around templates and cut out shapes until you have a total of:

Two branch pieces	One large bird back
Four small bird pieces	Two large bird wings
Two small bird backs	Two large leaves
Four small bird wings	Two small leaves
Two large bird pieces	

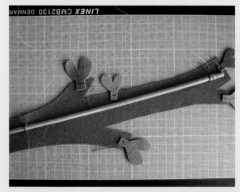

• Paint eyes and tummy on a side A and a side B of felt bird pieces. Set aside to dry completely.

• Take doweling or bamboo and tightly secure nylon thread, about an inch in from each end. Leave a long loop to hang the mobile.

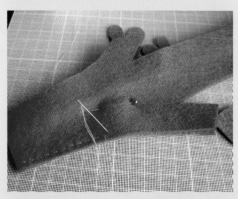

• Attach the doweling or bamboo to the inside of one of your branch pieces. Do this by sewing a few securing stitches around the wood and through the felt, on the outermost side of the doweling or bamboo. This will prevent the nylon thread from slipping over the end of the wood!

• On the same piece of branch felt, attach the leaves where you'd like them with a couple of basting stitches.

• Start to sew up the branch using small running stitches, starting from the bottom left. Once you are half done, start to stuff the sticking out branches with toy stuffing – you want them firm but not rigid. Continue sewing up the branch, stuffing as you go. Make sure the nylon thread remains outside of the branch and doesn't get caught up in with the stuffing.

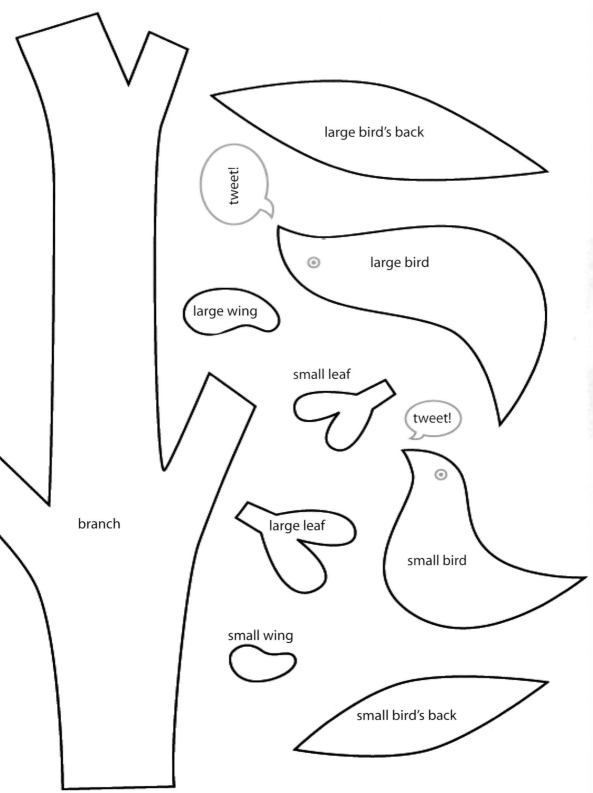

• Once the bird pieces are dry, start decorating with stitches!

• Large bird – French knot
Bring your needle and thread through to the front of the felt – holding the thread taught, wrap it twice or three times (this will vary the size of the knot) around the needle. Making sure you hold the thread 'behind' the needle as you push down, stitch down through the felt near to where you came up. Make sure you don't go back through the same hole, as your knot will disappear!

• Small bird 1 – Satin stitch
Make parallel straight stitches to fill a section of fabric. Put in a few 'guide' stitches to help you keep going in the same angle.

• Small bird 1 – Ermine fill
Make a vertical straight stitch then overlap with a cross-stitch. This makes a six-pointed star.

• Sew wings to side of birds using Fern stitch.

• Make three radiating stitches, all going down through a central point. Continue in a line along the wing.

• Start to sew bird pieces together using small running stitches. To do this, hold one bird piece and one bird back together at the beak end. The pieces don't at first appear to line up, but as you keep holding, stitching, moving along a bit and holding, stitching etc, all will be revealed.

• As you are sewing the two curved edges together, the fabric appears to buckle, when in fact it is two flat pieces of fabric becoming a 3D thing! Once you reach the tail, the two points should meet up exactly, if not, a bit of trimming won't hurt!

• Take second bird pieces and repeat, only this time start at tail end and finish up by the beak. Repeat again sewing along bird tummy beak to tail. About an inch from the end, fill with toy stuffing and a few toy beads.

• These give the birds some dangle weight – not too much, just enough so that they hang nicely. Repeat this with other two birds. Finish by sewing a piece of cotton through the backs of the birds, to suspend them from the branch.

• Attach birds to branch. You might want to try tying the branch to something while deciding where to place the birds. Use safety pins to get the birds into position so they balance nicely.

• Then sew the birds' thread into the branch, on the same side as you have small stitches showing from securing your doweling or bamboo.

Christa Rowley
CRAFTY LIKE A FOX!

Crafty Like a Fox! produces craft kits including cross stitch, rug hooking and paint-by-number kits that reference feminism, nostalgia and pop and folk culture.

www.craftylikeafox.ca
www.craftyfox.blogspot.com

'As a child growing up in the suburbs, there weren't many avenues to creative expression. I enjoyed craft kits, but stuck to drawing because it allowed me to follow my own designs. I soon realized that, although I loved making clothes and various domestic objects, my tastes would never fly in my status quo town. After a move to art school in the big city, I began to feel like there was a place for me and my work. My enthusiasm, however, was soon squashed by the sense of alienation I felt from the pretentious and exclusive gallery scene. It was simply a game I could not bear playing. Having worked as an art instructor for small children, I became inspired by their liberated approach to creating. This inspiration, coupled with my leanings toward anti-commercialism and the promotion of handmade goods, caused me to look toward craft, namely textile based work, as a new art medium and hobby. I began to use textiles to illustrate my own work, which examines women's role in popular and folk culture, to much praise. Many people were surprised to see craft used as a method to communicate ideas as opposed to images of geese and ballerinas. I began to wonder why it was so rare for one to see craft used to make cool stuff, or for those less artistically inclined, why were there no cool craft kits? Within three weeks of asking myself these questions, Crafty Like a Fox! was born. I now run my business part-time while creating a body of textile based art, and I have dreams of helping to replace the visual art scene, which caters to the rich and pompous, with the more grass roots and non-elitist craft community as a means of visual communication in our culture.'

Sophia Loren Cross Stitch

Christa Rowley

Following the instructions, and sticking to the pattern, make this cute cross stitch of Hollywood screen legend Sophia Loren.

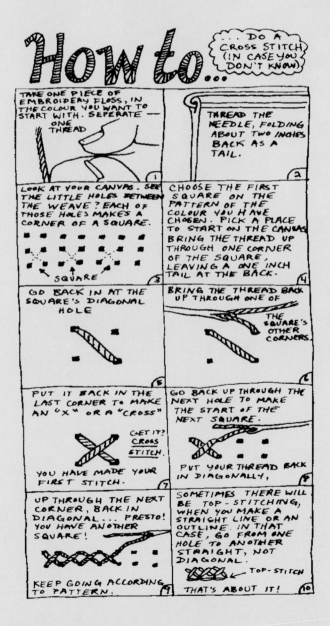

MATERIALS

- Cross stitch fabric
- Embroidery thread in the following colours:
  - orange
  - brown
  - black
  - fuchsia
  - pink
  - yellow
  - blue
- Frame (optional)

- - - black top stitch
--------- brown top stitch

Dress Yourself

You might be devoted to buying organic, Fair Trade food but do you think about the production of your clothes? As well as the fact that an objectionably cheap labor force is being used to produce cheaper and cheaper clothes, we are also amassing a huge surplus of unused and barely worn clothing. Those that do take the time to consider the way their clothes have been produced are beginning to choose a more ethical alternative, to reclaim traditional skills, giving them a modern twist and making their own clothes and accessories.

The Handmade

Most people would agree that it is a great feeling to be recognised for our achievements but in everyday life and work this seems to rarely happen. We get on with the routine of our lives, at a steady pace that offers little room for recognition. Craft is a simple way to show yourself and others what you are capable of – and you can learn new skills. It makes you feel proud when you make something. People appreciate the handmade now more than ever – where once it was commonplace, with everyone making their own clothes, now it is unexpected. People used to make all their own clothes but now it is refreshing to see evidence of the maker in an item. Those little clues that this was not made by a machine but by a person with experience and feelings, make all the difference to a garment. It doesn't need to be perfectly produced, this is not the point. Is it so much more special just because it has been made by hand.

Laura Harris
LAURAFALLULAH

Laurafallulah designs and makes one off handmade handbags, purses and accessories and is currently branching out into fashion and home accessories design.

www.laurafallulah.com

'From as far back as I remember I have always been involved in arts and crafts. My pre-schoolteachers used to have to drag me away from the drawing boards, at junior school I belonged to the after-school knitting club, and by the time I was at senior school I started to make my own clothes. Since then I haven't stopped, and have carried on my crafting as both a hobby and as part of my education. At University, I studied Constructed Textiles where I learnt how to use a knitting machine, how to weave and also types of fabric appliquéing. I specialize in weaving and to include my love of fashion I decided to make my final collection of fabrics into handbags. This really got into my blood and felt so natural to me so after graduating I knew this was the path to go down. Now I make and design one off handbags and purses as well as corsages, brooches and other types of accessories. Two years ago I started selling at markets in London and then started selling over the internet. I now sell over my site and also have a shop on www.etsy.com as well as selling at shops in London. I will try my hand at anything, which is why I love sewing because there is always something new to try. I love to take commissions from people and working alongside them to create a mix of their perfect bag with my kitsch style. Crafting has become more popular because it is no longer just seen as just making toilet roll covers or as something your grandmother does. With the rise of crafting groups and DIY craft fairs, craft is involving a much younger crowd of people. Crafting is the best way to spend your time as it is relaxing, productive and creative – what more can you want?'

Floral Wrap Skirt

Laura Harris

For many crafters, making your own clothes is a way of refusing to be a part an often oppressive clothing industry. Some might not find their body shape or needs catered for within mass-market uniformity. Others simply enjoy the art of making their own clothes. Luckily you can cater for both of these elements at the same time. Laura Harris is skilled at designing and making her own clothes. Her wrap skirt can be made for any size so there are really no restrictions. The design includes appliqué – the technique of embellishing an item with cut out fabric shapes. You can use this technique to decorate anything, from revamping an old T-shirt to decorating a jacket you sewed yourself.

MATERIALS

- Main Fabric
- Scraps of other fabrics for appliqué flowers
- 1m of green fabric
- Ribbon
- Bondaweb
- Tape measure
- Sewing machine
- Iron

INSTRUCTIONS

How Much Fabric You Need

- First you need to work out your measurements. To find out what width of fabric you will need, measure what will be the waist of your skirt. To do this you will need to take your tape measure and, holding it on your left hip, wrap it all the way around you clockwise till it overlaps and ends up on your right hip. Remember to add on an extra 10cm for seam and hemming allowance. On a UK size 12 this should be about 155cm or 61". Now you need to measure the length, this is for an under the knee length skirt. Simply measure from your hip to the bottom of your knee and then add an extra 2cm for hemming allowance. This can obviously be altered for a different length of skirt. This measurement will be the length of your fabric. For the ribbon you will need to add around 120cm more than your waist measurement or enough to go around the fabric twice. Always buy a little extra of the ribbon as this can be trimmed afterwards.

The Pattern

• The first thing to do is hem all of the sides starting with the edge that will be on the inside of the wrap, the left. To do this simply fold over the edge twice and sew down about 2mm in from the edge. Then on the opposite side you will need to fold it over twice again but this time it will need to be a wider hem of 2.5cm. Then stitch one row down at 2cm in and then a second row at 2mm in from the edge.

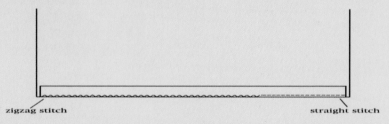

zigzag stitch   straight stitch

This will create a heavier hem making the outside edge hang really well. The next hem is the top, which will feature the ribbon. Turn over your rectangle of fabric so that you are looking at the face of your skirt, the wider hem will now be on your left and the other two hems will be at the back. Simply fold over the top of the skirt once onto the front and pin. Then take your ribbon and pin it, top and bottom, over the hem so that it covers it. At this point make sure that you have more of your ribbon on the side with the wider hem, you will need 50cm on the opposite side so the rest should hang off of the side with the wide hem. Sew along the top and bottom to secure the ribbon in place. Next you will need to put in the darts at the back of the skirt so that it fits neatly around your waist.

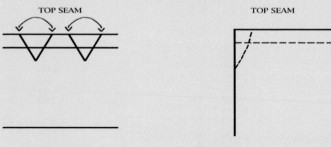

BACK VIEW

The easiest way of doing this is to put the skirt on a mannequin that is set to the right size but you can do it on yourself. Put the skirt on, pinning it where the ribbons meet. It will be very loose at the back, this is where you will need to put two darts in to bring it in. This will differ slightly from person to person but all you need to do is pinch in the fabric at the waist so that it fits in neatly and pin the tops. Take off the skirt and transfer the darts to the inside so you will have two flaps on the inside of the skirt top. Hold onto the spot where the pin is and on the back of the skirt fold the fabric from top to bottom. Sew down in a triangle from where the pin is to the edge of the fabric this should be at least 10cm. Copy this on the second dart.

You will need to cut a slit in the ribbon and top of the skirt so that you can bring the remaining ribbon through and tie it at the hip. To secure this slit it is best to sew a rectangle of zigzag stitching all the way around, so it resembles a large button hole. This will stop any fraying and also make the slit stronger.

Lastly you need to sew on a strip of green along the bottom to represent the grass. Cut two strips of fabric 10cm wide, and then sew these together to make up the width of the skirt. Place the seam at the back of the skirt and with the front sides facing, pin then sew along the edge. If you have an overlocker or serger you could use it at this point or on a domestic machine just zigzag stitch over the edge up to your straight seam to finish off the edge.

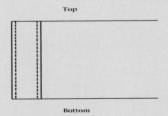

Top

Bottom

Then trim the side and follow the side hems down on this bottom section. The hem on the green section is a simple double-folded narrow hem but with two rows of stitching 1mm apart to add weight to the bottom of the skirt. You should now have finished the basic shape of the skirt, this is when you can add your appliqués.

Flower Appliqué

• This stylized flower appliqué is made by layering a smaller circle of fabric over a larger one. You will need circles in four sizes and two sizes of leaf. I used red and white patterned fabric but you can use whatever fabric you want for this part. Cut out a section of the bondaweb and iron the gluey side onto the fabric pieces. You should get instructions with the bondaweb but if not just put the papery side of it face down onto your ironing board and lay your fabric on top, then with a hot iron slowly iron the fabric. Make sure your fabric is suitable for a hot iron before doing this as some fabrics will melt or discolor with a hot iron. Cut out your circles from your bonded fabric and then peel off the paper back from the small ones and iron them on top of the larger ones. At this point I like to lay out my design onto my skirt so that I can move it around until it is perfect. You can pin out your design and then iron on each flower and leaf separately. After you have ironed on all of the design you will need to sew around each flower, the centres and the leaves. Plus from each flower sew a line of green thread down to the bottom green section to create the stalks.

Now wear your creation in public to make everyone jealous of this fabulous skirt. As I said before this can be made in any colour you want or you could try using different textured fabrics as well as patterns to create a different look.

You can also use this design to decorate existing items of clothing or accessories (see appliquéd bag, left). It would also work well along the bottom of a quilt or cushion. Be creative and put your own twist on a simple floral design.

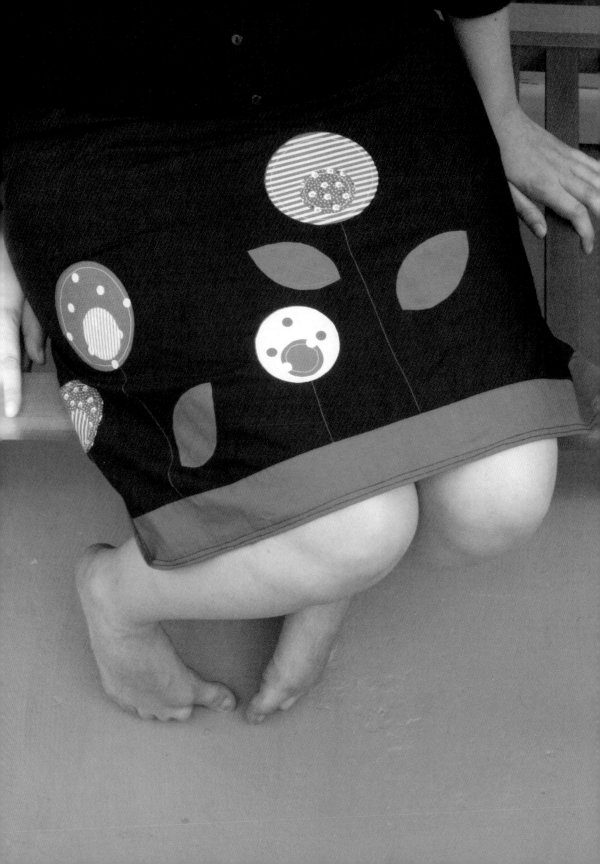

Amy Karol
ANGRY CHICKEN

Amy Karol is a crafter who has embraced the possibility of using the internet to explore her crafty side. She runs an art site to show her own art, textile work and notecards, as well as running her crafty subscription project club. Her blog, Angry Chicken is where she writes almost daily about her love of crafting. Her apron site, Tie One On, is where she writes about all things aprony and hosts a monthly challenge for people to make aprons following a particular theme.

www.kingpod.com
www.angrychicken. typepad.com

'I started sewing at around age three as my mother was always crafting and even as a child I had full use of her machine, it was never off-limits. I know I jammed up the thing really good a few times, but by the time I was five I was making my own small stuffed toys and doll clothes. I remember learning to crochet at six. I later studied art and went though a time when I felt like craft was not significant enough, and that unless I was showing my paintings in galleries, I was wasting my time. I got over that pretty quickly and embraced crafting again pretty hardcore after my first daughter was born. I think I am most happy combining the historical aspect of domestic arts, quilts in particular, and making them my own in a new way, like in the wall quilts I do – that are really much more like abstract paintings than historical quilts. My biggest influences now are old-time publications featuring quilts, needle arts and recipes. I love seeing the information laid out and organized, and realized this was the main reason I started my "mailorder" craft subscription club.

I think interest in craft has a natural ebb and flow with each generation. I do think that many crafters that I know have got on the craft bandwagon since they have had children and been at home a bit. It's such a wonderful feeling re-using clothes for quilts, altering things, or making toys for your children. Craft is a way to express yourself and for me a way to feel alive. Also, there's a way to rebel by making your own things – not being told what to wear or how to buy, but doing it yourself.'

A Smock to Wear Out

Amy Karol

You will never want to take this smock off – it's wonderful to wear over dresses or jeans and can be used in the kitchen and while crafting to keep your clothes tidy. The simple construction makes it easy to sew and because it's based on your own measurements it will fit every body type. You can make it long or short – try adding pockets, ruffles, fringe or rick-rack to change the look. The closure in back is shown with buttons, but snaps, a hook and eye, or even velcro can be used if you prefer.

MATERIALS

• One piece of smock body fabric 58" wide x 26" long (this can vary depending on your preferred length)
• 1/4 yard contrasting smock band and strap fabric
• Four buttons
• Matching thread

GENERAL NOTES:

Seam allowances: 3/8"
Pre-wash all your fabric before sewing

INSTRUCTIONS

• Measure your ribcage right under your armpits. Add 6" to this and this will be your overall band length. The band width is 7".

• Cut this out and iron up ½" hem on each long side of the band. Iron in half (longwise – right sides facing together) and stitch ½" from the edge, closing short edges of band.

• Turn, poking out the corners and press.

• Make the straps by sewing tube out of a 5" x 45" piece of strap fabric. Sew right

sides together leaving ends open, turn tube right side out, press with the seam centred. Fold in half and cut, creating two equal lengths of strap pieces.

• Cut out the smock fabric and hem the two sides by folding up ¼" twice and stitching the edges.

• Repeat on other side. For bottom hem, fold up ¼" and then 1" and topstitch.

• Create gathers on the top edge by measuring in 16" from each smock outside edge and marking with a pin.

• Stitch a gathering stitch between the pins, ¼" from raw edge. This is the longest stitch length on your sewing machine. Leave long tails and pull one thread creating gathers in the middle of the smock until the fabric pulls up and is the width of the smock band.

• Attach the smock to the band by placing the band right sides together and stitch ¼" (along folded line).

• Turn and press. Now pin the finished hem toward the inside, covering the raw edges on the inside and stitch from the front through all layers just above the band seam, creating a topstitching line. This should catch all layers on the inside. Fit the smock (a friend is very helpful here) by pinning it around your ribcage loosely and then pinning on the straps. You want the straps to hold it up, don't make it fit too tight around your ribcage.

Mark where it feels comfortable in the back and then pin the straps.

• Pin the straps to the front, making sure they extend over the whole band, top and bottom.

• Topstitch along the length of the band, catching the straps on the inside. Sew a second seam from the inside, anchoring the straps to the bottom of the band, right over the topstitch that is already there. Cut off any excess strap material.

• Add buttonholes and buttons to the back, overlapping the band as need to make it fit right. Remember that you will want extra room if you plan to wear this over many layers.

Secret Sewing Circles

When I was a little girl and my mother went to her sewing circle I thought that it was just about sewing. I think I must have thought that they went for the fun of playing with all the fabric and threads and making pretty things. I couldn't then have realized that throughout history women have gained so much more than that from sewing circles.

Needlework always been seen as an acceptable activity for women. It is closely connected to taking care of the home and the family. Women were permitted to go to sewing circles by husbands who may not have otherwise wanted their wives socializing without them. After all it was just the harmless company of a group of women working on their needlework alongside one another. For women, it was often a chance to socialize without feeling they were neglecting their families. They were given the chance to gather together and share experiences, tell stories and be supported by the other women.

Sewing circles have even been used as a cover for more revolutionary activity. Some women held resistance meetings while under the guise of simply meeting to sew. They might have been sewing with their hands but their minds and voices were free to plan.

Chandra Sweet
HONORABLE MENTION

Once you have been sewing for a while you will realize that you tend to hoard all types of fabric. From little off cuts, left over from finished projects, to metres of fabric that you bought on a whim and now can't think what to do with. Chandra Sweet has come up with a simple way to use fabric scraps to make unique brooches. So dig out your favourite scraps and your trusty sewing machine and make yourself some new accessories.

www.honorable-mention.com

'Crafting has always been a love of mine. When I was little I used to make Barbie clothes out of pretty much anything I could get my hands on. A lot of socks were destroyed to make Barbie a new gown. Recently, I found all these crafty websites and wanted to join in. So I bought a sewing machine and taught myself to sew. My grandmother helped me with basic stitches. I decided to add my handmade stuff to my vintage clothing website (www.sweetcouture.com) and people really liked it. I've now opened a site just for my handmade wears (www.honorable-mention.com) and couldn't be more excited about what I'm going to make next.

Crafting has always been popular, but because of the internet you are now able to show your work to a bigger audience. There are sites dedicated to hipster crafting so now you can see all these awesome people doing just what you are doing. Now crafters are the cool kids.'

Flower Scrap Brooches

Chandra Sweet

MATERIALS

• Approx eight fabric scraps in various colors, designs and blends (all around 2"x 2" in diameter) for the petals
• Fabric piece 2" x 3" for the leaves
• Strong glue
• Flat pin back (to attach to the back of the brooch)
• Scissors
• Pins
• Sewing machine and thread

INSTRUCTIONS

• For the flowers, take a piece of fabric and using your scissors cut scallops to create a circle. Repeat with seven or eight different fabrics in various sizes. The circles should be between 1" and 3" in diameter.

• Take the piece of fabric you'd like to use for the leaves and cut an oval that's pointed on the ends, resembling a leaf. It should be about 1 ½".

• Take the scalloped pieces and place them together, overlapping them to create a flower.

• Then, take the leaf piece and place it behind the flowers so it's just sticking out. Pin it and go to your sewing machine.

• Take the pin out and going in circles sew all the pieces together.

• Now, taking a piece of fabric, cut out a little heart that will fit in the back area of the pin back. Put glue on the heart and place it on the back bar of the pin back. Then, attach the heart to the back of the flower in the middle, covering up some of the stitches you just made.

• Let the glue dry and then pin your brooch to your favorite jacket!

Stock your Sewing Box

To get started I recommend filling your sewing box with the following:

• A thimble to protect your fingers when tacking long seams or quilting.

• Plenty of threads of different colours and types. When buying sewing thread, select one make from the same weight and fibre as the fabric you are stitching. Mercerized cotton has a smooth surface and should be used for cotton and linens. Polyester is finer and can be used for mixed fabrics. Choose a darker shade than the material you are sewing if the exact match is not possible.

• Skeins of embroidery thread can be removed from their paper loops and wound onto cardboard spools for ease of use.

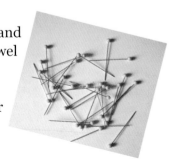

• Several pairs of scissors, each useful for a different purpose: a good pair of dressmaking shears, with long heavy steel blades and angled handles; pinking shears give a decorative zigzag edge; Sewing scissors, smaller with straight handles.

• Hand sewing needles come in various sizes for different tasks. Medium length for general sewing and tacking. Shorter needles for slip stitch and quilting. Crewel needles with a long eye designed for embroidery.

• Pins. Stainless steel dressmaker's pins can be used for most fabrics. Glass-headed pins are best for wool and other thick material.

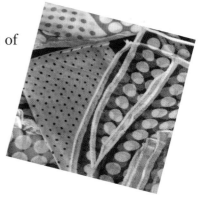

• Collect all the little pieces of trimmings, scraps of lace and ribbon.

• Buttons.

• Dressmaker's carbon paper.

• Iron-on transfer paper for drawing outlines for embroidery onto fabric.

• Interfacing to back and strengthen fine or woven fabric.

• Fusible bonding web for joining fabric and appliqué.

• A tape measure.

• A sewing machine is also useful. (This doesn't have to be an expensive investment. You can buy an expensive computerized machine with advanced features but all you really need is a basic stitch.)

I have always been a scavenging sort. I hunt for bargains in junk shops, charity shops and car boot sales. I pick up broken junk abandoned in the street, always with the aim of transforming the unwanted into something functional and beautiful. I have ended up with a houseful of junk. 1960s chairs – a perfect shape, just need recovering. A beautiful yellow 1950s Formica table that just needs a clean and a bit of glue to fix a wobbly leg. I love the potential of objects, seeing beyond their current state and imagining something new.

Many clothes can be constructed from any fabric, and you will no doubt want to be choosy over something you'll be taking time over. Picking a fabric that you like doesn't have to involve buying new materials however. There are so many wonderful fabrics available, already sewn into different shapes and sizes. By recycling these, cutting them apart and sewing them into something new you can have a whole new wardrobe. We are constantly encouraged to buy new clothes by the fashion industry, to wear the current styles and get rid of the old. Designers have the creative control, the consumer is only able to choose from a narrow selection. These choices are marketed as a form of creative decision, you can use clothes to express your individuality, but there is no avoiding the fact that we are buying into someone else's vision of fashion. This constant selection and reselection of clothes has led to a vast textile waste. Consumers are encouraged to buy more and more as the discarded clothes pile up. What better to way to reject this cycle than use these unwanted clothes to create something new. Garments that you will love to wear in the knowledge that you recycled and customized them yourself. If you don't want to customize your clothes alone you can work with others. San Francisco artist, Helena Keeffe started organizing the garment-remake exchange. In a craft version of a pen pal system, participants send out items of clothing they no longer wear with a Polaroid of themselves wearing it and a note on how they feel about it to a stranger in another city to remake. In return, they receive a garment to transform through cutting up, sewing together, modification and embellishment (www.garmentremake.com).

Ilona Jasiewicz
CRAFTERNOON

Ilona Jasiewicz is a London-based editor who uses her newly developed sewing machine skills to create exciting soft furnishings, clothing and accessories out of vintage fabrics. Though she studied fashion design at college, rather than focusing solely on clothing she prefers applying her imagination and resourcefulness to a range of different projects – enjoying sewing in particular because it yields instant results.

'I've always preferred quirky, personal items to mass-produced so I guess it was only a matter of time before I stopped buying things other crafters had made, and started making my own. A decade ago, I studied fashion design for a couple of years, made a small collection, sold a couple of pieces, and then didn't sew again for about eight years. In 2001, I became involved in organizing Ladyfest London, and met tons of brilliant crafty ladies who inspired me to start crafting again – going back to sewing was the obvious choice. Friends have tried to teach me to knit, or crochet, but I resisted, mainly because I am too impatient and like to see instant results: a cushion cover takes thirty minutes to make and can transform a room. Last year I got a sewing machine and I haven't looked back. Vintage fabric has yielded cushion covers, headscarves and plastic-bag holders, the scraps make lavender sachets for my wardrobe. I've made a bag, dresses, hideous silver hotpants (for performing with 1960s go-go dancers the Actionettes, www.actionettes.com) and curtains.

Current projects involve me thinking of items I really want and then sewing them. I'm planning to make a coffee cosy (a padded, Velcro-fastening wrap for a cafetière), a fabric cover for my card holder so it doesn't get scratched up and a fabric belt. I co-run Crafternoon, an occasional afternoon club in London for crafters, featuring workshops, cakes and DJs.'

Vintage Pillowcase Dress

Ilona Jasiewicz

Vintage pillowcases are a fantastic source of vintage fabric. Why not transform this little piece of vintage style into your own unique dress or top?

MATERIALS

For a top to fit a 36" bust and 40" hips you need:

• One standard size pillowcase with envelope closing
• 8' of ½" wide bias binding in a bright, clashing colour
• Sewing machine, threaded up in a contrasting colour (I used white)

INSTRUCTIONS

Choosing Your Pillowcase

• Find a nice vintage patterned pillowcase, and hold it up against you, with the open end hanging down and the closed end level with your chin. If you're making a top you may want to shorten the length of the case (you can use the excess fabric for a matching headscarf). If you are making a dress, you will probably have to let down the fabric at the envelope end of the pillowcase (there are usually 4-5" of fabric making up the envelope of the pillowcase). I'm 5' 3" and a standard pillowcase makes a just-above-the-knee-length dress, so be prepared to wear your mini with pride if you're taller.

Making the Straps

• Measure from the top of your shoulder to below your armpit in a straight line – this will probably be 9" or so. This measurement will be used for the straps of your dress/top. This may seem a lot but you'll be making a wide-ish hem at the top of the dress/top for the ties to go through.

Side view

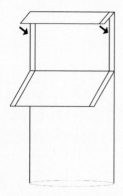

Fold over 1 ½"

Thread bias binding

Scrunch the fabric

• Cut open the closed end of the pillowcase. Then make two slits (these are your armholes) either side of the new opening along the side seams.

• Now slip the pillowcase on, and see how it looks. Shorten if it's too long, and if it's too short and you've run out of fabric to let down, add a contrasting piece at the hem.

• If the dress/top needs hemming, give it a ½" hem.

Sewing Together

• Iron your bias binding in half lengthways and cut in half. Cut in half again – use one piece for each armhole – and carefully sew it around the open slits, which will be armholes. End the bias binding just before you get to the top of each side – this will make it easier to sew later.

• Fold over the top 1½" of the fabric, and press. Using a narrow seam allowance, sew this down to the wrong side of the fabric on the front and back of the dress/top, making sure you leave an opening at each end to feed the ties through.

• Take the remaining two pieces of your bias binding and cut it in half. You can leave it just ironed or sew it down (I prefer this, as it looks pretty). Put a safety pin in one end of the bias binding and feed it through the tube of fabric you just sewed.

• Once you've done this on both sides, tie bows and scrunch the fabric a bit to the centre.

Susan Beal
SUSAN STARS/SUPER CRAFTY

Susan Beal is a fully-fledged crafter. Her handmade jewelry and A-line skirt kits can be found at www.susanstars.com. And you can also find her craft projects and writing here. She writes a monthly craft column at www.westcoastcrafty.com, and the many projects that her collective is up to can be found at www.pdxsupercrafty.com.

'I have always loved making things and as a teenager I made myself jewelry out of everything I could find – restringing broken costume necklaces on dental floss, adding hardware store bits to old chains. After I finished college, I started making jewelry again and got to go to a two-week silver-smithing workshop in the mountains. I loved every minute of it. But when I found a jewelry school in Portland, Oregon with a six-month program it sounded absolutely dreamy – so I visited, fell in love with the city, and moved across the country to take classes.

I started selling my work in 1999 to a few small boutiques, and learned to sew on an old thrift-store Singer in 2000 – right around the time I discovered www.getcrafty.com. Suddenly I was meeting tons of cool crafty girls, hosting naked lady parties and craft-ons, and sewing up a storm. I started designing a small line of handbags and skirts in addition to my jewelry, and eventually managed to quit my day job so I could craft more or less full-time.

In 2003, I started meeting up with a handful of other creative businesswomen in Portland and we formed a collective called PDX Super Crafty. In early 2004, we were asked to write a book – *Super Crafty: Over 75 Amazing How-to Projects!* – and now I'm working on my second book, on jewelry making. I also write for *ReadyMade, BUST, Venus, Cutting Edge, Adorn* and *CRAFT* magazines, plus doing a monthly column online. It's busy and overwhelming, but I wouldn't have it any other way.'

Vintage Slip Camisole and Travel Bag Set

Susan Beal

Turn a plain cotton or nylon slip into a pretty camisole and handy drawstring travel bag by adding a few ribbons and trims. This simple sewing project is easily customizable, too – just use your favorite colors as accents and embellish it with any design you like. This project uses a narrow bright green ribbon under delicate white lace for a feminine, vintage-inspired look on the top, and a bolder pattern of green ribbons to decorate the bag. This project is quickest with a sewing machine, but you can also stitch it by hand.

MATERIALS

• An old slip that fits you well
• Thread
• Felt scraps in two colors
• Three buttons
• Scissors
• Iron
• Pinking shears
• Straight pins
• Sewing machine (optional, but recommended)
• Needle and thread for hand-sewing
• Measuring tape
• Elastic guide or large safety pin
• Ribbons and laces of your choice

This project used:
• 5 yards of wide green ribbon (A) to embellish both the camisole and bag
• 2 yards of delicate cotton lace (B) to embellish the camisole
• 1 yard of 5/8" wide ivory satin ribbon (C) for the camisole's straps
• 1 yards of 1" wide pale green patterned ribbon (D) to embellish the bag
• 2 yards of 1" wide ivory grosgrain ribbon (E) for the bag's drawstring

Making the Camisole

• To start, decide how long you will make your camisole – you can compare it to a top you already have or try the slip on and mark it. Add one extra inch to the length to account for the hem. I wanted mine to be 15" long from the center of the V-neck to the hem, so I measured down 16" and cut the slip there. After you cut it, set the bottom half aside for now – it will become the travel bag.

• To create the felt flower embellishments, first cut two pieces of ribbon A to form the stems – one 6" long and one 4" long. Pin them to the front of the camisole, off center and about 2" apart and hand-sew them on with small stitches.

• Cut out two oval shapes in your first felt color (I used ivory) with pinking shears – the larger one 1" x 2", and the smaller one 1" x 1". Then cut two slightly bigger oval shapes out with scissors in felt color #2 (I used green).

• Layer the two flower shapes together and pin them in place over the top of each ribbon 'stem'. Hand-stitch them down and add a button to the center of each one.

• Now form the hem. Turn the raw edge at the bottom of the camisole under ½" and press it neatly with the iron. Then turn it under once more, hiding the raw edge within the fold, and press it flat, pinning it every two or three".

• Using a sewing machine (or backstitching by hand) stitch the hem securely, discarding the pins as you go.

• Pin a piece of lace B to the bottom edge of the hem, overlapping it slightly at one side. Machine-stitch or hand-sew it onto the hem.

• Now accent the bodice of the camisole with lace and ribbon. Pin ribbon A all along the neckline and below the chest. You can baste it on by hand or with a sewing machine – the layer of lace will cover it so the ribbon just peeks through. When you reach a corner or angle, fold the ribbon under into a triangle shape

• Pin the lace over the ribbon and stitch it on securely, turning it under at each side, and folding it when you reach an angle. I used my machine to sew it on, once above and once below the ribbon. Then ornament the center of the V-neck with a single button.

• Last, you'll replace the old lingerie-style straps with ribbon C – try the top on and measure how long the straps are (mine were about 15"). Cut two pieces of ribbon and pin them in place, and then machine-stitch them down securely.

Making the Travel Bag

• First, you'll form the drawstring casing at the top. Turn the raw edge under 1" and press it flat. Then turn the hem a second time and press it, pinning it every few inches as you go. Starting at one side, machine-stitch it all the way around, leaving an opening about 2" wide to put the drawstring into. Backstitch at the beginning and end of the seam.

• Pin ribbon A horizontally along the bottom edge of the slip, about 2" above the edge, and stitch it on (I used a zigzag stitch on my sewing machine).

• Pin ribbon D on about ½" above the first ribbon and stitch it on. (I machine-sewed it with two seams, at the top and at the bottom.)

• Turn the bag inside out and pin the bottom edge together, and stitch it closed to form the bottom of the bag.

• Now you'll make the drawstring. Take the 2 yard piece of ribbon E and pin a 2 yard piece of ribbon A to it. Stitch it on (I used a zigzag stitch on my sewing machine) and then fold each end of the ribbons under and stitch them down. (You can also use a plain ribbon, of course.)

• Using the elastic guide or large safety pin, insert the drawstring into the casing and put it through all the way around and then pull it out the other side. Now you can easily open and close your bag – just tie a bow to secure it when you travel.

Melissa Alvarado, Hope Meng, Melissa Rannels
STITCH LOUNGE/SEW SUBVERSIVE

San Francisco's Stitch Lounge offers a programme of imaginative craft classes for people wanting to express their individuality by creating their own clothing and clothing accessories. Its organizers are the authors of *Sew Subversive,* a book about making fashion your way. Whether it's embellishing or customizing shirts, skirts or pants to make them uniquely your own, they have creative ideas for everyone. The book is full of refashioning projects, like turning T-shirts into skirts, sweaters into hats and leg warmers and pants into hipbelts.

www.stitchlounge.com
www.sewsubsersive.com

'The three of us have been friends since childhood – we have nearly sixty years of friendship between us. Melissa A started off by making scrunchies in her mother's sewing room. The lessons were mainly trial and error; she learned via many broken needles that no matter how many times you try to shove six layers of denim and elastic through the machine, it just won't go. Melissa R has been crafting since she was old enough to mold peanut butter play dough and attributes her proclivity toward creativity to her mother, who never gave her coloring books, but provided unlimited blank paper and crayons. She started refashioning early in life by turning sleeves from her mother's blouses into cocktail dresses for her Cabbage Patch Kid. Hope has been creative and crafty her whole life, dabbling in photography, dance, illustration, painting and just about anything else that requires right-brained thinking. She started sewing six years ago, when her acceptance into a local belly dance troupe required her to make her own costumes! Hope hasn't put down the needle and thread since.

Although we've been sewing and crafting since we were young lassies, the three of us really started getting into it again when we reunited in San Francisco after college. We went to the Burning Man festival together six years ago and every year since our costumes have gotten better and more elaborate! Three years ago, we opened Stitch Lounge in San Francisco, the first drop-in urban sewing studio. The space and community that is Stitch has expanded our sewing world and freed our creativity.'

Flutter Sleeve Refashioned T-shirt

Melissa Alvarado, Hope Meng, Melissa Rannels

MATERIALS

• One T-shirt
• Sewing machine and thread
• Scissors

INSTRUCTIONS

Cutting Your T-shirt

• Cut the following pieces from your T-shirt:

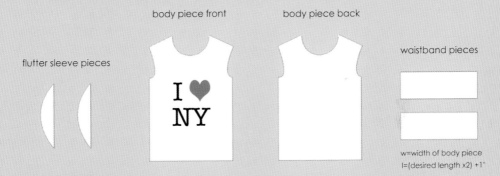

flutter sleeve pieces

body piece front

body piece back

waistband pieces

w=width of body piece
l=(desired length x2) +1"

Sewing Back Together

• Fold the waistband pieces in half and pin to the bottom of the body pieces. Sew the waistband to the body piece.

waistband

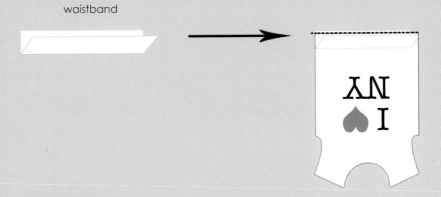

• Sew the body pieces together on the sides and the shoulders.

Flutter Sleeves

• Fold each flutter sleeve lengthwise. Pin the flutter sleeve pieces to the armholes loosely.

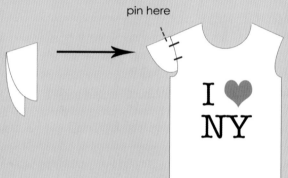

pin here

• Sew the flutter sleeve pieces to the armholes. Cut the flutter sleeves at the shoulder.

cut here   cut here

• If desired, use a zigzag stitch and finish the edges of the flutter sleeves.

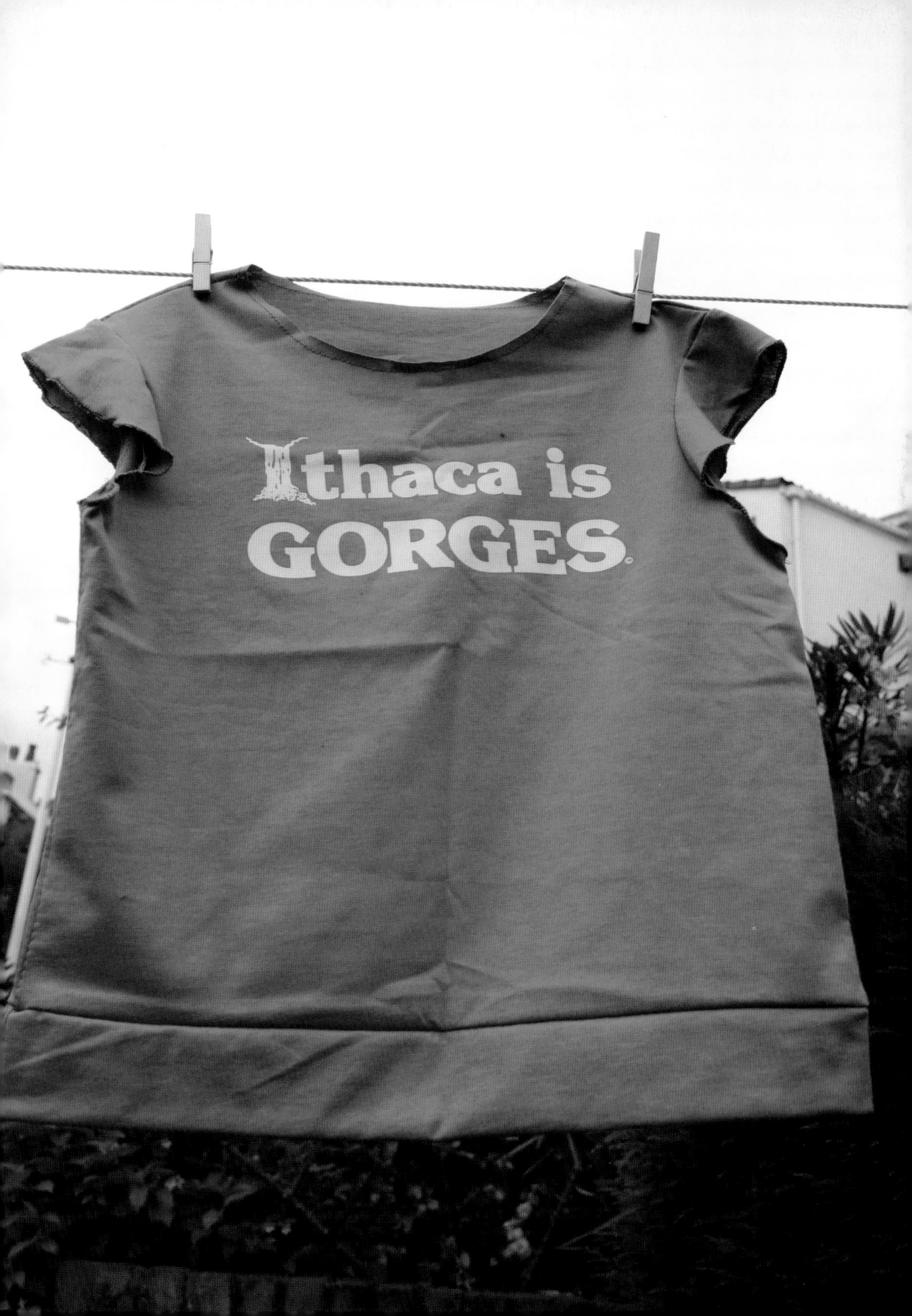
Ithaca is
GORGES

Melissa Dettloff
LEKKNER

Melissa Dettloff has been transforming unwanted T-shirts into new items for years now. She takes inspiration from the T-shirt's original design and then turns it into something different. The perfect form of recycling.

www.lekkner.com

'I learned how to sew as a kid – my mother sews, and her mother sewed. I started hand-sewing pillows and toys and got onto the machine sometime in high school and began to make clothing. We had a serger in the house at the time and I began to use that as well. The serger became an important tool in my explorations into T-shirt reconstruction: it gives the perfect finish for T-shirt/knit seams. I started reconstructing T-shirts for myself a long time ago. I would find T-shirts that I liked at the thrift store, but they never fit right. So I fixed that. I began doing custom reconstructions for the masses in 2003.

Crafting has always been around, but more "under the radar". I think it has surfaced more of late in large part because of the internet, and the relative ease it allows in gaining an audience for your project.'

T-shirt Tote Bag

Melissa Dettloff

Everyone will have at least a few unwanted T-shirts just calling out to be turned into something new. Melissa Dettloff shows you how to quickly transform a vintage T-shirt into a cute bag with just a few snips and stitches.

MATERIALS

• One T-shirt
• Cotton (woven – not stretchy) fabric: either 2/3 yard (of standard width, 45-54") for both the lining and the strap; OR, ½ yard (of standard width) for the lining plus 2/3 of another fabric for the straps (this is if you want the strap to be a different fabric from the lining, like my sample). Thrift store-found fabric is great for this!
• Fusible interfacing, medium weight: 1 1/3 yards. This makes your tote sturdy and durable!
• Velcro: 2" piece
• Optional: if you want to decorate the outside of the tote with appliqué (like I did), you'll need scrap pieces of fabric for that, in addition to some Heat & Bond or Fusiweb, which will adhere the fabric to your tote.

INSTRUCTIONS

Pattern pieces
Front/back of tote: 12" x 14"
Sides of tote: 4" x 13"
Straps: 4" x 22"

It's a good idea to cut these pieces out of tissue paper, Kraft paper, newspaper, etc and use them as your pattern for cutting.

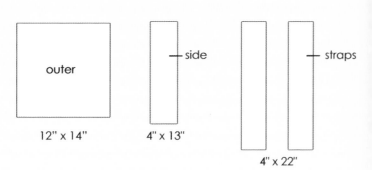

outer

12" x 14"

— side

4" x 13"

— straps

4" x 22"

• Choose and wash a T-shirt that has a graphic on it that you'd like to be seen carrying around!

• Split the T-shirt up the sides with scissors.

cut up the sides
so you can lay the
t-shirt like this:

• Lay the front/back pattern piece onto the front of the T-shirt and arrange it in the way that you'd like the graphic to end up on your tote: centered, off to the side, on the bottom, etc. Cut around the pattern piece – I recommend using a rotary cutter, weights and cutting mat for all pattern cutting.

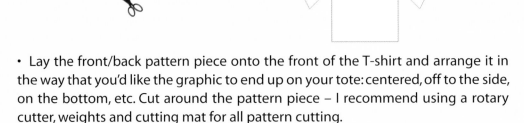

or

dotted line=pattern piece
laying pattern piece so that
the graphic ends up where
desired

• Next, you will cut the outer back and outer sides of your tote. Arrange the pattern pieces on the leftover pieces of the T-shirt so that you can cut one more outer piece and two side pieces.

• Now cut your lining: cut two of the outer pieces and two of the side pieces from your lining fabric.

• Cut your straps: cut two of the strap pattern piece from your fabric.

• Cut your interfacing: you'll need four of the outer pattern piece, four of the side pattern piece, and two of the strap pattern piece.

• Press all of the interfacing onto the back of all of your tote pieces.

• Fold one strap in half long-ways, right sides together, and stitch along the longest edge, taking in about a ¼" seam allowance. (You'll be taking a ¼" seam allowance for all stitching on this project.) Do this for the other strap. Turn them inside out when done, with a loop turner. Press them flat. Now you've got straps!

• At this point, you will have to decide if your tote will have appliqué details on the outside, like the sample (I added the fabric heart). If so, decorate the front of your tote as desired: using scrap pieces of fabrics, first press the Heat & Bond or Fusiweb to the back of the fabrics. Then cut them into the shapes you desire. I cut out a heart. Then peel off the backing of the Heat & Bond or Fusiweb, and press the shape onto your tote, wherever you want it. Appliqué stitch around the shape, using a zigzag stitch of the width you desire.

• Now comes the construction of your tote. Take one side and one outer piece and lay them right sides together, with top edges matching/even. Stitch, taking a ¼" seam allowance. Now take the other side piece, and stitch that to the other side of your outer piece, right sides together. Lastly, take the remaining outer piece, and stitch that to your two side pieces, right sides together, top edges even again.

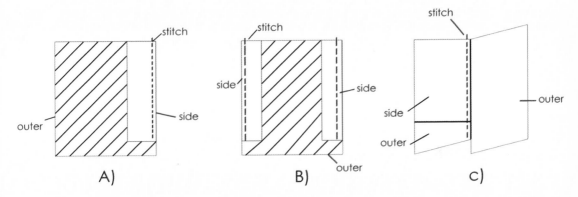

A)   B)   C)

• Stitch along the bottom, right sides together. Then stitch the corners, bringing the bottom up to meet the sides.

• Repeat the last two steps for your lining.

• Insert your lining inside your outer tote, wrong sides together. Baste stitch along the top edge to keep them together. Fold down to the inside about ½", pin and press. Fold down another 1" to the inside, press and pin. Now stitch along the edge of this fold.

• Pin your straps to the inside of your tote, with each end approximately 2" from the sides. Stitch your straps down, with an X. Fray-check (this a product which will seal the seams) the cut edge of the straps, which will prevent fraying.

• Stitch the velcro tabs, one on each side, to the inside-center of your tote.

Scott Bodenner
BODENNER STUDIO

The Scott Bodenner Studio tackles a wide variety of design jobs, but the focus is on making textiles for interiors.

'My earliest crafting memory is making Valentines with my sister. Really I think she made the Valentines and I played with glue. Later in school I was teased for my non-commercial Valentines made of doilies and construction paper, but I knew I had the flyest of heart shaped hand-outs. Since then I have been making as many things as time allows.

My career as a textile designer allows me the chance to create on a day-to-day and industrial scale. I feel fantastically lucky to have been able to find and develop this market niche.

Current studio projects include a collection of outdoor fabrics, working as a designer for an American and a Swiss mill, and a salesman for mills in Switzerland, India and Turkey. We have the honor of inclusion in the book *Craftique* edited by Tsia Carson and to be frequent contributors to www.supernaturale.com.

As we are more and more inundated with products in a wide range of styles, I think as consumers we start to yearn for the understanding of a maker's hand in what we surround ourselves with.'

Felting: Wool Alchemy

Scott Bodenner and Shawn Merchant

Using a color palette reminiscent of a farmer's field, this blanket is made entirely from recycled materials. Alchemists tried to change lead into gold. We are able to change woolens into felt using nothing more than a washing machine. Felting causes the yarn's fibers to mesh together so they maintain their bias and stretch, but will not unravel when cut. You can turn anything woolen (including cashmere and alpaca but not acrylic) into felt. Here we'll outline the basic techniques and show you how to make a blanket. From there you can take felting wherever you can imagine.

MATERIALS

- Sewing machine and thread
- Washing machine

For our project we gathered wool fabrics I have been hoarding:
- One twin size army blanket
- Two Harris Tweed sport coats
- One open weave wool blanket
- One crocheted sweater dress
- Some silk and wool fabrics
- Some random sweaters and suiting fabrics

INSTRUCTIONS

Making Your Felt
When you felt a wool fabric, what happens is that the temperature changes and agitation causes the curly barbed wool fibers to alternately straighten out and then spring back and lock together. They get all tangled up resulting in a tighter, sturdier piece of fabric. The easiest method of felting is to throw sweaters into a washing machine for a normal cycle (hot or warm wash, cold rinse). A small amount of soap (try 1/8 of what you might normally use) will also aid in felting. In the washing machine, hot water felts more than warm water. Similarly, a long cycle felts more than a short cycle. If sweaters aren't felted to your desired thickness or smallness, they may require multiple washings, but be careful.

Felting as Tailoring

If you are shrinking a baggy sweater and it is sort of close to what you'd like, stop before it gets way too small. Sweater arms often become too short during felting. One solution is to wrap them in a 5cm wide strip of a non-wool material. Looping, and knotting each loop seems to work best since it won't come undone in the machine. This technique is similar to tie dying, so you could choose areas you want to pucker out and not felt, tie them off and throw that into the wash.

Felting gives you freedom because exposed edges won't unravel. You can tie them with loops of yarn, or crochet them together, or sew them with a machine or by hand. Felted material can now be cut and sewn into new garments, quilts, rugs, hats, anything requiring the durability, flexibility, density and beauty of felt.

Note: Make sure the woolens don't matter too much to you since felting is something of a voodoo art, and there is always a chance of over felting. It is also possible that your wool just won't felt at all.

Color Bleeding: Wools often bleed so make sure that you combine colors that will look good if they tint each other.

Shrinkage: Shrinkage occurs more in the length than the width of a knit. Ribbing, at the bottom and sleeves of a sweater, tends to felt less and sewn seams often don't felt at all.

Making Your Blanket

• Felt all your wool fabrics until you are pleased with all the pieces you produce.
• If the colors of the pieces do not fit into your color scheme, you can dye them to match. For this blanket, the dress, open weave blanket and silk and wool fabric were over dyed to bring them into the color range. I like to use Aljo acid dye (www.aljodye.com) in the hot washer cycle.
• Next, cut the fabric into 20cm wide strips being sure to cut out any holes or seams.
• Lay out the strips to make sure the color placement is random but even.
• Next machine sew the strips into one gigantic length using 1.5cm seam allowances.
• Iron the seams flat. (Ironing the seams means this new blanket looks great whichever side is showing).
• Cut the length of the pieces into sections of the size you'll need for a queen size bed and sew them together.

Jamie Peterson

Jamie Peterson specializes in crocheting purses and handbags from old plastic bags. She also knits and crochets a variety of wool items: unique hats, custom mittens or gloves, bracelets, animals, *porte-objets*, etc. Most of her designs come from experimentation, and she seldom repeats a design unless asked.

www.members.cox.net/bagbags

'I have always felt the instinct to make something useful or pleasing from scraps found around the house. Where most people see garbage, I see possibility. As children my brother and I were hands-on during playtime. Later we went our separate ways: he began assembling model airplanes while I stitched and folded and glued little characters and created worlds for them to inhabit. Origami, sewing and needlepoint were my favorite crafts and I found immense pleasure in these activities because they yielded precious material artefacts that others could also appreciate. I quickly found that gifts to friends and family were better if I made them myself, because what was available in stores was never exactly right. The person (or machine) who made those products didn't know my father, or sister, or best friend, so how could they possibly know what color or what image would work best, what size?

Later in life I discovered knitting and crochet and immediately became obsessed with crochet. I was thrilled with its simplicity and limitless possibility: the idea that I could create any conceivable form with just a stick and some string. About five years ago I was on a rock tour on the west coast. I often knit or crochet "merch" for the band to wear or sell at the shows. During one leg of the tour I had run out of yarn. There was a piece of saran wrap left over from a sandwich on the floor. In a flash I picked up my needle and was working the saran wrap into a wristband. In that moment I decided to make use of the seemingly useless plastic bags that accumulate everywhere, thereby killing two birds with one stone.'

Little Red Plastic Bag

Jamie Peterson

This project calls for as many old plastic bags as you can get your hands on. You will never look at used plastic bags in the same way. You don't need to give them to someone else to recycle, you can transform them yourself – into a stylish and practical accessory.

MATERIALS

• The number of bags you need depends on the size you want, both the size of the bag and the size of the stitch you are planning to use. The medium-size tote bag described below is made with about 30-35 bags, using a 16mm needle for the body of the bag, and an 11mm needle for the handles.
• Crochet needles (11mm and 16mm)

INSTRUCTIONS
For a rounded, medium-sized tote bag

Prepare the Plastic Bags

• Cutting the bags takes almost as long as crocheting the bag. Sometimes I like to cut them one at a time, as I am crocheting, and other times I cut as many as I need for an entire bag all at once.

• First, flatten the bag. Cut a thin strip off the bottom and a thin strip off the top below the handles. (These pieces can be thrown away or saved to make decorative shapes to attach later.)

• The bag should now be a wide tube-like shape. Starting at either end of the 'tube', cut the bag spirally. If this is confusing, imagine you are transforming the tube into the form of a spring, or slinky. Start by cutting into the base at an angle. Continue to cut while maintaining as fixed a width possible at each turn. Once you have cut all the way up the bag, you should have one continuous piece of plastic yarn.

• You can control the thickness of the weave by varying the width of the strip. For a medium-size tote bag, the width is approximately 2.5 – 3". (In theory you could cut a very fine thread and make rather delicate pieces!)

• Connect bag end to bag end with a double knot, or granny knot: right over left, left over right. While crocheting you can hide the excess knot thread into the stitch as you go along.

Crocheting the Bag

Warning: this project may take a bit of elbow grease, especially if you use thicker bags.

• Chain stitch 39. Keeping the chain straight, slip stitch into the first chain stitch. Now you have a ring.

• Single crochet in a round for 5 rows. Starting on the second row, half-double crochet into the top two loops for a tighter stitch.

• At the beginning of the 3rd row, increase a stitch. Then increase a stitch at the halfway point of the same row (at about 18 stitches). It's best to eyeball the halfway point because the material tends to be irregular.

• Increase one at the beginning and halfway point of the 4th row.

• 5th and 6th rows crochet normally.

• At the beginning of the 7th row, decrease one, half double crochet one, decrease one. It's best to decrease by grabbing two stitches (each stitch grab double loop) rather than skipping a stitch.

• When you reach two stitches before the halfway point of the 7th row (at about the 16th stitch) decrease two stitches again in the same manner.

• Decrease in the same manner for rows 8 –12.

• Flip the bag inside out and stitch the bottom seam of the bag. You can do this without having to cut the thread: hook through two loops of one side of the bag, hook through two loops from the opposite side, yarn over, and pull the thread through both sides. Work your way to the left or right (depending on which side you are working on), continuing until you have stitched the entire length of the bottom, closing one end of the bag.

• Tie off. Turn bag right side out.

Crocheting the Handles

• Decide where you want to put the handles. For the tote bag I inserted them 4 stitches in from the sides. Switch to the smaller needles. You can still use the same thickness of yarn.

• Tie on the right side, grabbing two loops.

• Starting with the hole you tied onto, single crochet two stitches (right to left) grabbing two loops each stitch.

• Chain stitch until you have the length of the handle you like. I used 22 stitches for the bag handles.

• Single crochet three (left to right) into the edge of the left side of the bag, calculating distance from the edge to balance it out with the right side (if you started 4 stitches in on the right side, start at stitch 7).

• Single crochet back along the chain stitch that you have just stitched, grabbing the backside loop of the chain.

• When you get back to the beginning, single crochet into the edge of the bag on the left of where the handle meets the bag to make it more solid, then tie off.

• Repeat for the other handle.

Linda Permann
ADORN MAGAZINE

Linda Permann is the founding Craft and Decorating Editor for *Adorn* Magazine, a new publication all about fashion, crafts and embellishing life. She also hosts her own site where you can find a variety of craft projects including crochet necklaces, children's toys and sweet and sassy brooches to add that finishing touch to an outfit.

www.adornmag.com
www.lindamade.com

'My early memories of craft are rooted in church and family. My grandmother was a very crafty lady and she sewed each one of our Sunday dresses by hand. There were four girls in my family, so this was no small effort. I remember going to the fabric store and picking out fabric, zippers, buttons and notions in anticipation of each upcoming holiday. I loved spending these shopping days with her and my sisters. The excitement of seeing something made entirely the way you want it from raw materials you choose yourself has always stayed with me, and is one of the main reasons I craft. While growing up, I made crafts at Sunday school – everything from finger puppets to felt banners. For me, being good at arts and crafts was a source of pride when I didn't always feel like I fit in.

In my sophomore year of college, my next door neighbour showed me www.getcrafty.com. I was amazed. I met a group of wonderful women from all over the world who I still connect with each and every day six years later. After moving to New York, I was able to personally meet many of these crafters, and we started regular craft nights. Whereas craft was once a way for me to be secure in myself, to work alone and feel proud of my accomplishments, I started to bring it out of my house and connect with other people.

Now that I design and make crafts for a living, my after-hours crafting is back to being a very personal, solitary activity meant only to fulfil myself. To me, crafting is about making something that I feel a want or need for, that doesn't already exist in the way I want it to. Craft is control, pure and simple.'

Vintage Button Jewelry

Linda Permann

Vintage buttons are a quick and easy way to add a little unique vintage style to any outfit. You can easily pick them up cheaply in thrift stores and charity shops. Make this pretty necklace and bracelet using the buttons you find.

MATERIALS

- Six to eight 1" vintage buttons in desired colors (per necklace/bracelet)
- Six to eight ¼" buttons, clear
- 24 gauge beading wire (gold)
- 12" gold chain (necklace only)
- Necklace clasp or hook (I used an ear wire for the 'hook' and a jump ring)
- Pair of needle nose pliers
- Wire cutters

INSTRUCTIONS

Threading Buttons

- Cut approximately 16" length of beading wire.

- Lay out arrangement of vintage buttons as desired on table (the clear buttons will act as spacers on the backside of the vintage buttons).

- Thread beading wire into one hole of first button (with the right side of the button facing you).

- Next, thread wire end through other button hole, and through one button hole of small clear button (with the wrong side facing you).

- Turn the necklace over so the right side of the small button is facing you.

- Thread the wire end through the other hole of the small clear button and through wrong side of the next vintage button.

- Turn the necklace over so that the right side of the vintage button is facing you.

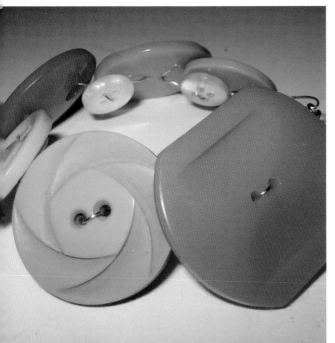

• Thread wire end through the other hole of the second button and through the wrong side of next small clear button.

• Repeat this threading process with six more buttons (the number of buttons is variable depending on desired length).

Finishing the Necklace

• Thread the end of the wire through 6" length of chain and twist wire end tightly.

• Trim the wire end and conceal in button. Repeat this step for the other side.

• Attach a necklace clasp to the chain ends of the necklace with pliers.

Finishing the Bracelet

• Fold over approx 1" of wire on one end of buttons to form loop.

• Grasp top of loop with needle nose pliers and twist together tightly, leaving an open loop at end.

• Conceal wire end in button, trimming if necessary.

• On other end of buttons, thread wire through hook (or ear wire) and back, twist wire together.

• Trim end, conceal in buttons.

Host a Naked Lady Party

This isn't as risqué as it sounds. Invite all your friends round to your place for a party instructing them to bring with them all their unwanted clothes to swap. All those garments in the back of their wardrobes that are too small, too big or those bought and never worn will soon have a proud new owner. At the party, everyone tries on each others clothes and chooses some to take home. It's a perfect way to recycle – you get something you want without spending any money and clothes don't end up being thrown away when they are no longer wanted by their original owner – and it's fun too!

Changing Color

If you find the perfect vintage garment or piece of fabric that is just the wrong color you can easily change it to suit your taste. Simply choose your new color from the vast range of dyes made to permanently dye your clothes inside your washing machine and pop it in your machine with your garment or fabric to change its color. This simple technique means that you don't have to be restricted by original colors.

Craft doesn't have to be just about fabric, thread, wool or paper. It's about using any material that enables you to create something new and some innovative crafters have begun to mix technology and more traditional crafts. Whether they are adding coloured lights to clothing or making instruments out of old electronic toys, there really are no limits. The beauty of electro craft is that it opens up the crafter to a whole new range of possible creations – fairy lights, buzzers and chip boards have never been so tempting!

I bet you never thought you could make a microphone to amplify that old classical guitar that's lying in the back of the cupboard. For many people the very thought of trying to re-wire an electronic circuit is terrifying. The fact is that none of this stuff is rocket science, anyone can do it with a little basic guidance. Electro craft is no longer the domain of geeky teenagers with too much time on their hands, everyone is getting involved.

Some electro crafters modify existing products, transforming them by giving them new and often unexpected uses. Others create entirely new objects and circuits from scratch. The thing to remember is that electronics needn't be complex. Using some simple techniques you can make anything you choose.

The projects in this chapter serve as an introduction to electro craft. They have been designed by skilled crafters with the aim of introducing everyone to the potential of mixing craft and technology. There are invaluable step-by-step instructions for each project, but as with all crafty endeavours, never be afraid to bend the rules, to experiment, and to adapt a project to your own needs or preferences. All you need is the confidence to be inventive and the contributors to this chapter should set you well on the way...

Eleanor Partridge
CRAFT ENTREPRENEUR

Eleanor Partridge runs Craft Entrepreneur, a site dedicated to helping crafters publish their own independent books and zines. It compiles interviews with crafty business people and their various books and projects they have made.

www.craftentrepreneur.com

'I remember crafting when I was young and have always enjoyed making stuff with my hands. I used to make popsicle stick puppets and houses out of milk cartons. In high school, I experimented with clothes – adding strips of fabric to my pants. Like most crafters I have tried most things such as painting, screen-printing, crocheting, knitting, decoupage projects and whatever else catches my fancy. In 2004, my husband suggested that I should write an ebook about crafts. I started planning the ebook in the Fall of 2004 and finished it about nine months later. It was about sixteen crafty home décor ideas. My next book featured my long time favourite Christmas item, holiday string lights. My most recent project was a compilation book of handmade hair accessories. It is the first compilation book that www.craftentrepreneur.com has published and I'm cheerfully crossing my fingers for its success, and for the books that will follow. I hope to see more independent craft books and articles to get people excited about the world of self-publishing.

I think crafting has risen in popularity recently because people are tired of buying mass produced, soul-less junk. And because it's no longer considered dorky, like it was in most of our parents' days. I think more and more people are getting into crafting now because there's many possibilities for self-expression and individualism. Also, it's fun!'

Hanging Spheres

Eleanor Partridge

Have you ever wondered what to do with your fairy lights once Christmas is over? Eleanor Partridge has come up with a quirky way to transform them into something different to use all year round. Using common household items – two simple colanders – she has created a design for unique lamps to create a glamorous party atmosphere.

MATERIALS

- One 35 bulb strand of green lights
- One 35 bulb strand of purple lights
- One 35 bulb strand of amber lights
- Six white plastic colanders
- Twist ties
- Strong string
- Tool cutters
- Contact cement
- Three ceiling hooks
- Extension cord

INSTRUCTIONS

• Cut the bottom out of three of the colanders with utility cutters.

• Use twist ties to attach lights to the colander.

• Twist tie the lights on four equal parts at the top of the colander. The light should be twist tied to the top colander so it takes all the weight and there will be no threat of the bottom falling off.

• Poke a string through the holes and tie five knots in the ends, so the lights don't fall through.

- Add a second same length string across the other way.

- Put contact cement on the four handles of the colander.

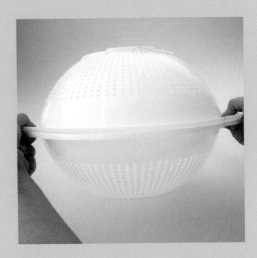

Hanging Your Spheres

If you want to hang your spheres from the ceiling, you will need to screw one ceiling hook into the ceiling for each sphere. Make sure that you screw the hook into a wooden beam or use a rawl plug to ensure that your spheres will be secure.

Warning

Care must be taken when using your spheres. Do not leave the lights unattended when they are on. Do not put fabric or paper next to or over the lights, this could be a flammable hazard. Never use the lights near water. If in doubt, refer to the light manufacturers' safety instructions.

- Wait 15 to 60 minutes before pressing the colanders together.

Alison Lewis
I HEART SWITCH

SWITCH is a personal video blog produced by Alison Lewis. It aims to inspire young women to create with electronics by presenting people, projects and ideas related to design, fashion and home accessories. These are cute creations that show electronics isn't just for the boys.

www.iheartswitch.com

'I don't see myself a crafter; instead, I see myself as an artist and maker. I tend to look at crafty as a state of mind and picture any "craftiness" I may have as part of my approach. Crafty is how I see materials, how I approach expressing an idea to others or insights on how to put things together. By making electronics crafty, I hope to make them friendly and more approachable to a wider audience of people who may not otherwise want to work with electricity or computation. Any craftiness I have comes from my grandmother, Alice Merryman. Alice, now one hundred years old, still paints, crafts and quilts. Her ability to use materials of the earth and work with historically famed "crafts" and the decades she's been working makes her the crafter in our family. It will take decades for me to make the impact she has. I spent many summers with her in Clinton, Arkansas as a young girl and she introduced me to painting and her tenacity to make things. My grandmother does corn shuckery, a Native Indian craft where they take dried corn husks to make baskets, seat bottoms, dolls and more. She published a booklet in the late 1960s called the 'Shuckery and Corn Artistry', was celebrated at the Smithsonian Arts and Crafts Fair as a symbol of Indian Craft and showed her projects at the Worlds Faire in 1964. The craftiness that people may see in me comes from a history of sewing and painting and my absolute need to create and share what I've learned with others. I combine my concepts of an artist and crafter into making technology more approachable and "crafty" to a new generation.'

Lovie Circuits

Alison Lewis

Lovie circuits are two plushie dolls that light up when they 'kiss' or are together. They can be made large or small, depending on your style. Keep them small if you want to add them to a backpack or keychain or make them large if you want something you can hug and display!

TRADITIONAL MATERIALS

- 1 yard of fabric (Fabric A)
- Fabric scrap material for heart cut out (Fabric B)
- Partly translucent white rayon or cotton to disperse the glow from the LEDs (Fabric C)
- Stuffing/Polyfill
- Fabric Scissors
- Paper Scissors
- Four magnetic buttons – make sure you buy both the (+) positive and the (-) negative
- Needle/thread
- Sewing machine (optional)
- Two four-hole buttons
- Permanent marker
- Hot glue gun w/glue

ELECTRONIC MATERIALS

- Two 3V batteries
- Two plastic key covers (found at local hardware store) – the solid ones, not ringed shaped
- Two blinking red LEDs (Light Emitting Diodes) or you can use any LED which needs power between 2.6 and 3 volts. These can be found at local electronic store or search online
- Conductive thread or super thin jewelry wire (thin enough to sew with)
- Soldering Iron and Solder
- Electronic tape
- Mylar (or use a candy wrapper)

INSTRUCTIONS

For large Lovie, increase the size in a copy machine to 220% larger or desired size. Measure and use the side pieces as guides to how big you want it to be.

PATTERN

Makes two small lovies
(approx 3" x 3" with 1/8 seam)
For Large Lovie:
increase size to 220%
Use a 1/4" seam
Remove flaps from pattern
Use seam on #5 for closure

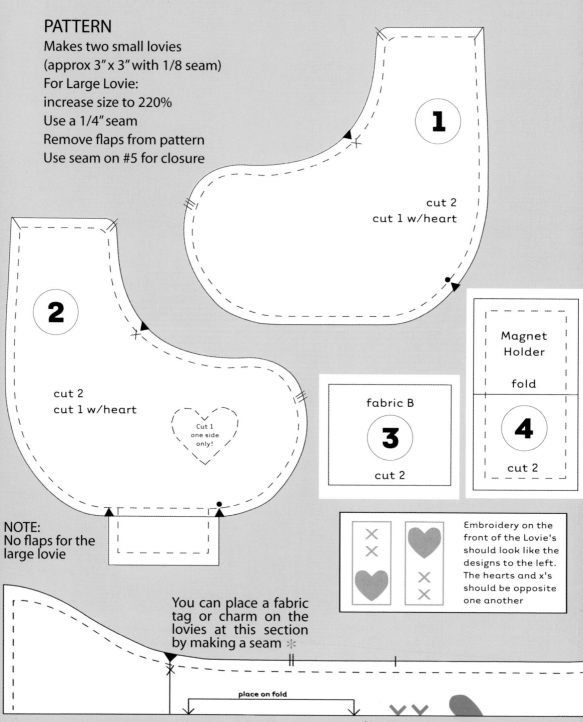

1

cut 2
cut 1 w/heart

2

cut 2
cut 1 w/heart

Cut 1
one side
only!

3

fabric B

cut 2

Magnet
Holder

fold

4

cut 2

NOTE:
No flaps for the large lovie

You can place a fabric tag or charm on the lovies at this section by making a seam ✳

place on fold

Embroidery on the front of the Lovie's should look like the designs to the left. The hearts and x's should be opposite one another

(x's and heart embroidery reverse for second Lovie)

If you are using an old pillow (as we suggest) then use a seam ripper along the edges to open it up. Take out the stuffing and set aside and iron the top pieces flat for use as Fabric A.

Layout and cut out the Lovie pattern on Fabric A. Cut two.

NOTE: Do not cut out the heart shape yet.

NOTE: If you want a really fat Lovie, it helps to cut part 5 on the bias. You can then stretch this part out as you stuff later.

Layout and cut out the heart background color on Fabric B.

The Heart
For both Lovies cut out the heart shape. Again, make sure they are on opposite sides so that they both face front when the Lovies 'kiss' (see middle photo above on p109). An alternative is to put the hearts on the Lovie Butt or wherever you want!
• Cut part 3 from Material B (the heart material).
• Line up the square shape over the heart shape and make sure there is at least 1/4" overlap.
• Sew, by hand or on machine Material B to Material A around the heart. Use the heart shape as the guide.
• If you like, you can do a tight zigzag around the heart shape for a secure decoration or just leave it with a stitch.

Sew
The Lovies are sewn together somewhat like a sleeve for a shirt. Start with piece 5 making a round part and attach the two Lovie sides with a base stitch.
• On piece 5 turn under ¼" on each end and iron down (this is where the snaps will be).
• BASE stitch the ends together (you'll be pulling it apart later).
• With the fabrics inside out together sew on both sides of the Lovie to piece 5 following the notches around the edges. (Suggestion: make a wide base stitch like you would a shirt sleeve to get out the wrinkles before sewing the final stitch).
• Sew up ¾ of the way on both sides of piece 5 where the base stitching lies. You should have at least 2½" of base stitching left in the middle of the curve.
• Remove the base stitching from the center of the 2½" curve.
• Turn the Lovie right side out and inspect for any wrinkles or sewing errors and make adjustments.
• Turn the Lovies inside out again.

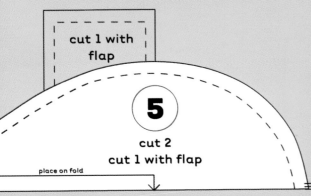

cut 1 with flap

5

cut 2
cut 1 with flap

place on fold

Blinking Light

You will have one LED for each Lovie strung through a four-hole button with the thread attached to the (+) positive and one to the (-) negative side of the LED. See diagram below.

• Put the (-) negative leg of the LED in one hole of the button and the (+) positive side of the LED in a hole diagonal from it.
• Use needle nose pliers to bend the ends of the legs around and into a u-shape so it can go into the hole next to the leg.
• Mark the corresponding holes with a permanent marker (-)(+).
• Set it aside for a moment

ADD the ELECTRONIC THREADS

It is very important that the threads for the two 'x's and the thread for the 'heart' or the LED shape never touch each other. That means every thread from the 'x' and the LED need to be totally separate and with different thread. Use the diagram for sewing the threads to the battery holder and the LED. These act as wires and connect your Lovie to the battery and to the LED.

• First sew the top 'x' shape then stitch down the seam to the base area.
• Leave some slack in the thread (about 3–4") and stitch or wrap it around one side of the key holder about four times then knot it off on the outside of the battery holder (see diagram p114).
• Mark this side of the key holder with a (+) sign in permanent marker.
• Sew the bottom 'x' making sure the threads don't touch the top 'x'. Then sew down the opposite seam to the base of the Lovie.
• Leave some slack in the thread (4") and sew the thread in a loop around the (+) marked hole of the LED/button combo. Also, wrap the thread around the (+) positive legs as well. You want to make sure that the thread does not touch any other leg or item on the button or LED but is firmly surrounding the (+) positive parts by stitching through and around the button holes and legs.

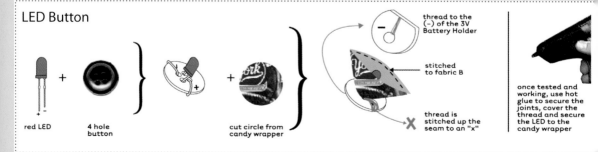

LED Button

red LED
4 hole button
cut circle from candy wrapper
thread to the (–) of the 3V Battery Holder
stitched to fabric B
thread is stitched up the seam to an "x"
once tested and working, use hot glue to secure the joints, cover the LED to the candy wrapper

• Knot and cut the thread. Use fray check in order to keep the threads secure.
• Take another piece of thread (about 5-6") and thread it in and around the (-) negative marked sides of the LED legs about 4-5 times.
• Then thread and loop the leftover thread around the other hole of the key holder and tie it off.
• Mark this side of the key holder with a (-) negative sign.
• Cut away any stray threads and wires.
• Test the circuit with a multimeter to be sure none of the (+) positive threads are touching any of the (-) negative threads.

TEST:
• Put in the 3V battery into the plastic key holder being careful that the (+) positive and (-) negative sides of the battery correspond with the (+) and (-) on the holder.
• Be sure none of your threads are touching.
• Take a straight pin and place it over both 'x's at the top of the Lovie.
• This should complete the circuit and allow the energy through to light up the LED
• If this does not happen go back through the directions again carefully. Again, make sure that all the threads are separate from one another and the (+) and (-) never touch.

FINISH
After the testing that the LED is working properly and the threads do not cross:
• Remove the battery
• Remove the straight pin
• Sew in the conductive threaded heart below the 'x's (again, with separate thread that doesn't touch anything else)
• Cut a circular piece of Mylar (for a cheaper option cut a circle out of a candy wrapper) and fit it around the Button/LED combo. The Mylar or shiny surface acts as a reflector to make the lights spread out evenly.
• Hot glue the Mylar to the button
• Sew the Mylar to the inside of the heart shape, leaving about ½" – 1" space from the light to the edge of the heart material (Trick: poke holes in the Mylar around the edges with a straight pin so it's easier to sew onto the fabric).

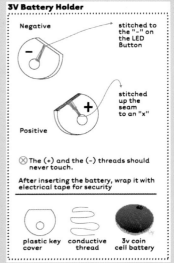

3V Battery Holder

Negative — stitched to the "-" on the LED Button

stitched up the seam to an "x"

Positive

⊗ The (+) and the (-) threads should never touch.

After inserting the battery, wrap it with electrical tape for security

plastic key cover | conductive thread | 3v coin cell battery

• Sew a pocket behind the two 'x's to hold the (+) positive side of magnet. Make sure the magnet doesn't wiggle around in the pocket and is perfectly centered over the two 'x's. (Note: If needed, make little stitches to hold the magnet centered in the pocket and over the 'x's).

• Stuff the Lovie, being sure to stuff between any threads so that the threads don't touch. This is especially important around the LED/button area and the 3V battery holder. Take the time to manipulate the stuffing to get the Lovies to stand just the way you want.

• Test the LEDs again. If there are any strings hanging or touching it may not work, so move the stuffing around until it seems to separate all the threads along the sides and around the battery area.

• The battery should sit in the middle bottom of the Lovie.

• Once it has been tested and is working properly, wrap the battery in electronic tape to keep it secure

• If you like you can add snaps to the Lovies or just sew them up.

• Test again

• Make your second Lovie making sure to reverse the order of the electronic thread 'x's and Heart. And be sure to put the (-) negative magnet in the second Lovie.

• Hold them together, they should be attracted to one another through the magnets and the Hearts close the circuits on each of the Lovies which turns on their hearts.

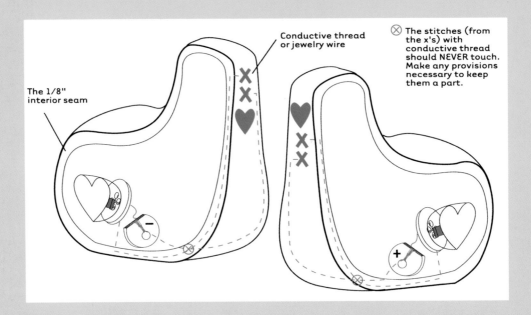

Syuzi Pakhchyan
SPARKLAB

Syuzi Pakhchyan of SparkLab is fascinated with the connections between fabric and technology, making imaginative and stylish clothes with audiovisual properties. SparkLab is an experimental research and design lab that lives in the intersection of culture, craft and technology. Working from the premise that technology can inspire and provoke, SparkLab creates a space for the cultural production of technologically crafted artefacts. It is a new platform that supports and reflects diverse attitudes and experiences and serves as a vehicle for communication of personal stories and cultural narratives.

www.sparklab.la

'As a designer, I am constantly making things or deconstructing them to see how they are made. My romance with craft and the craft community stems from my love of handmade objects. The idiosyncratic objects created by some shadowy artisan of genius or by the deliberate amateur to me is a continual source of inspiration. In my professional work, I tend to mix craft with industry, fusing handiwork with digital techniques and weaving the old with the new. My aspiration is to create work that can be read: work that is richly layered, personal and detailed that tells some lore or story. My interest in fashion stems out of a love for textiles, especially vintage textiles from the 1950s, 1960s and 1970s. I learned the craft of sewing through observation (being from the former Soviet Union, everyone in my family knows how to sew, mainly out of necessity) and by deconstructing garments to learn how they were made. My interest in technology, specifically digital electronics, probably too is via osmosis, having grown up in a household littered with soldering irons, microchips and voltmeters. With the development of virtual spaces and communities to share projects, ideas, tips and techniques, and most importantly, to receive accolades for your most recent creation, the internet has fuelled craft and the DIY ethos. Crafting is political. Every crafted object is pregnant with personal and social commentary, be it consciously or subconsciously. Through the very act of making these crafters are engaging in a political conversation with society.'

Light Bracelet

Syuzi Pakhchyan

This project is a lovely floral bracelet with its own light source. The flowers glow, powered by a simple circuit.

Go to www.sparklab.la/links.html for a list of online retailers and sources to purchase the electronic components.

MATERIALS

- Conductive Thread
- LEDs (Super Flux recommended) with a minimum 90¼ viewing angle
- 2 x 3V Batteries
- Two cell battery holder
- 9" x 3" thin piece of leather (or ultra-suede)
- 2 x 8.5" x 2.5" white diffusing fabric
- 9.5" x 3.5" patterned fabric for bottom of bracelet
- 2" of conductive velcro
- 6" of regular velcro
- 100-280 ohm 1/8 W resistor

TOOLS

- X-acto knife or rotary cutter
- Needle
- Sewing machine
- Alligator clips
- Pins
- Scissors
- Needle nose pliers
- Iron (for iron-on seam option). You can use iron-on seams if you do not wish to sew the bracelet. Sewing is recommended.

WHAT ARE LEDs?
LEDs are a bright light source which are low on power consumption and heat emission. Their are several types of LEDs out on the market. The one recommended for this project is the Super Flux wide angle square LED with a minimum of a 90¼ viewing angle.

WHY DO I NEED A RESISTOR?
Resistors are used to limit the current in the LED to a safe value so the LED will not burn out.

1. DESIGN

1.1| Design a pattern for the top leather (or ultra-suede) portion of your bracelet. Refer to www.sparklab.la/patterns for pattern suggestions. Keep the design a minimum of 0.25" from the edges.

1.2| Using an X-acto knife or rotary cutter, cut out your pattern. Some decorative hole punches may also be used to create a pattern.

1.3| You can either design a pattern for the bottom fabric of your bracelet, using an iron-on transfer to apply your image onto a piece of fabric or simply use a decorative fabric to your liking.

SUPER FLUX LED

LEDs are polarized which means that the current from your battery can only run through them in one direction. Therefore, in order to "wire" (in our case, sew) the LEDs properly, we need to determine the positive (anode) legs from the negative (cathode) legs.

The Super Flux LEDs have four legs – two positive (anodes) and two negative (cathodes). Since there are several varieties of these LEDs, the best way to determine which are the positive and negative legs is to wire them temporarily using alligator clips. This will be explained in section 2 "Testing an LED."

NOTE: If you are using typical 3mm or 5mm LEDS, typically the longer leg is the positive (anode) leg and the shorter, the negative (cathode). You can bypass the following section.

2. TESTING AN LED

2.1| Connect an alligator clip to the positive and negative terminal of your battery pack.

2.2| Connect one end of the resistor to the alligator clip attached to the positive terminal of the battery. Connect another alligator clip to the other end of the resistor.

2.3| Now connect one alligator clip to one leg of the LED and the other alligator clip attached to the negative terminal of the battery to another leg of the LED. MAKE CERTAIN THE ALLIGATOR CLIPS DO NOT TOUCH EACH OTHER OR ELSE YOU WILL CREATE A SHORT AND YOUR LED WILL NOT TURN ON.

2.4| If your LED does not turn on, switch the two alligator clips on the LED.

2.5| Once your LED turns on, take a red marker and mark the positive legs of the LED for future reference. The positive legs of the LED will be connected via the alligator clip to the positive battery terminal.

3. SEWING THE LEDS

3.1| Once you have determined and marked the positive and negative legs of the LED, you need to determine the placement of the LEDs.

3.2| Place a 8.5" x 2.5" piece of white diffusing fabric over your cutout leather or suede piece. Mark the placement of the LEDs on the fabric with a pen so you can sew the LEDs in your desired location.

3.3| We are going to sew the LEDs in parallel, meaning that all the positive legs of the LED will be sewn to each other and all the negative legs to each other.

3.4| Place the LEDs on the fabric with the positive legs (marked RED) facing in the same direction.

3.5| Pierce the legs of the LEDs through the fabric.

3.6| Turn the fabric over.

3.7| Using the needle nose pliers, gently bend legs of the LEDs flush to the fabric.

3.8| Using the conductive thread and needle, sew one of the positive legs of the LED to the fabric firmly.

3.9| Sew a straight line from one positive leg of the LED to the other.

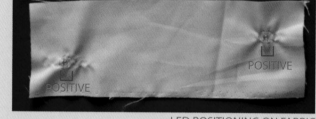

LED POSITIONING ON FABRIC

3.10| Repeat for the negative legs.

NOTE: MAKE SURE THAT THE CONDUCTIVE THREAD FROM THE POSITIVE AND NEGATIVE LEGS DO NOT TOUCH AT ANY POINT. THIS WILL CAUSE A SHORT AND YOUR LEDS WILL NOT LIGHT UP.

3.11| Test your connection. Using your Battery and Resistor Set-up (see "Testing an LED" Fig 2.1 & 2.2), connect the positive end of the battery terminal using an alligator clip to one of the positive legs of the LED (use one that you have not sewn too). Connect the negative end of the battery terminal to the negative leg of the LED.

CONNECTING POSITIVE AND NEGATIVE LEGS OF LEDS TOGETHER

3.12| Your LEDs should light up. If they don't, check to make sure that the conductive thread from the positive and negative leg is not touching at any point.

3.13| Place the fabric that will be your bottom layer of the bracelet right side down.

3.14| Lay the LED fabric right side up on top of the bottom fabric. The negative legs of the LEDs should be on top.

3.15| Fold over 0.25" hem along the width of the bottom fabric. Pin.

3.16| Pin the loop (soft) pieces of the conductive Velcro on the left side of the bottom fabric at least 0.15" from the edge.

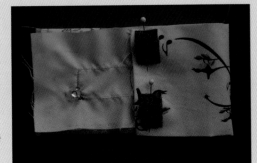

3.17| With the conductive thread, sew a line from the positive leg of the LED to the conductive Velcro, securing the conductive Velcro onto to the bottom fabric.

3.18| Repeat for the negative leg of the LED.

4. SEWING THE BATTERY PACK

4.1| Place the leather cover right side down on a table.

4.2| Place a 8.5" x 2.5" piece of white diffusing fabric right side down over the leather cover.

4.3| Place the battery pack with the positive terminal on top about 0.5" away from the right edge of leather cover.

4.4| Pierce the legs of the battery pack through the fabric.

4.5| Turn the fabric over.

4.6| Using the needle nose pliers, gently bend legs of the battery pack flush to the fabric. Mark the positive battery terminal on the other side of the fabric for quick reference.

4.7| Pin the hook pieces (prickly pieces) of the conductive velcro on the right side of the leather cover a little before the edge.

4.8| Lay the battery fabric right side up on top of the leather cover. The positive battery terminal should be on top.

4.9| Using the conductive thread and needle, sew the positive battery terminal to the fabric firmly.

4.10| Using the needle nose pliers, create a loop to both ends of the resistor.

4.11| Sew a line from the positive battery terminal to one end of the resistor.

4.12| Sew another line from the other end of the resistor to the hook conductive velcro, securing the conductive velcro onto the leather cover.

4.13| Sew a line from the negative battery terminal to the prickly conductive Velcro, securing the conductive Velcro onto the leather cover.

5. FINAL ASSEMBLY

5.1| Lay the leather cover and battery piece right side down with the positive battery terminal on top.

CONNECTING THE BATTERY AND RESISTOR

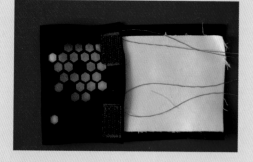

CONDUCTIVE VELCRO

5.2| Lay the bottom fabric and LED assembly (negative LED legs on top) on top of the leather cover right side up.

5.3| Fold the hems on all sides and pin down to leather cover.

5.4| Test your bracelet. When the two sides of the conductive Velcro touch, your LEDs should light up.

5.5| Once you've determined that you have assembled everything properly and your connections work, with the bracelet right side down, you can now sew the top and bottom of the bracelet together.

5.5| It is recommended that you use regular velcro on the right side of the bracelet and 3" of Velcro on the bottom so you can access your battery pack later to change your batteries.

VISUAL ASSEMBLY GUIDE

Although the visual guide is not necessary, it is a helpful tool to guide you along the construction process. Cut along the solid black line of the bottom and top layer guide. Fold both guides along the center dashed lines. Use it alongside the tutorial as a visual reference.

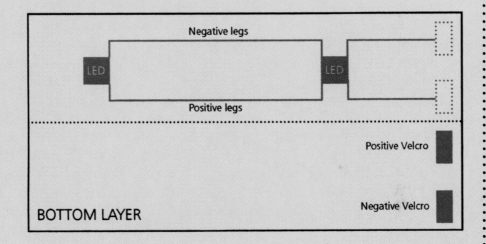

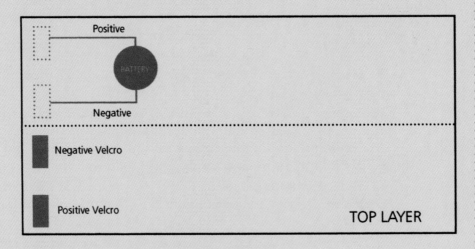

Ryan 'Zieak' McFarland

Ryan McFarland is an Alaska-based Parks and Recreation Director who dabbles in djing and web design on the side. He runs the site www.zieak.com as a showcase for his craft projects, design work and photographs. Whilst this is not a specifically commercial enterprise he is always willing to accept offers on any items of interest to his readers, but otherwise encourages other crafters just to browse – picking up ideas for new creations along the way.

'My origins in crafts really began in the Cub and Boy Scouts, where my focus became native crafts including beading and working with leather and feathers. I have dabbled in silk screening, graphic design, photography, and a few other visual arts. Taking electronics apart was always fascinating to me and I finally started to put them back together – but often in ways unintended by the original manufacturer. Now my crafting seems to center on reusing materials that would have been discarded or making children's toys into something functional or artistic for adults. I don't really think of what I do as "crafting" as much as it is "tinkering" and giving new life to old objects. I am an avid recycler and truly enjoy finding new uses for objects. For a year I have been collecting beanie babies at the local thrift store at about fifty cents each. I plan to make a beanie baby bag chair out of them by filling a large mesh or clear bag with them. I have also been collecting marble pieces from old trophies and hope to make a butcher block style end table top with the pieces turned sideways to conceal the holes drilled through the marble. Using some superglue, hot glue, a dremel tool and some wire hardly sounds like a craft – but that's what mine is – and it's in this book – so it must be some sort of a craft. But it sure isn't quilting. And I bet the local arts council wouldn't think of giving me one of their grants for a public art project. That's ok though – more people looked at one of my projects in the first week I posted it online than one of their murals is viewed in an entire year. People have copied my projects. People have offered to buy them – but I suggest they give it a try. It is just so satisfying to make something of your own.'

Nintendo Controller Optical Mouse

Ryan "Zieak" McFarland

www.zieak.com/projects/nintendo_mouse.htm
www.flickr.com/photos/zieak/sets/840733

Using a simple optical mouse and a Nintendo Entertainment System controller, you can make good use of a retro device. There is something almost elegant about the boxy controller. It isn't ergonomic, your hand lies on top of the mouse a bit flatter than on most modern mice but it is surprisingly comfortable.

MATERIALS

• An optical mouse (the fewer buttons and wheels the better)
• A Nintendo controller
• A few inches of phone line or other small wire
• Two small and low profile buttons
• Small screwdrivers
• Rotary tool (like a Dremel)
• Razor knife
• Super glue
• Marker
• Soldering iron and solder
• Hot glue gun and glue
• Wire cutters and strippers

INSTRUCTIONS

Taking Apart

• Unscrew the six small screws in the back of the controller and keep them for use later.

• Remove the circuit panel. Keep this too as you might need parts of it later.

• Clean the controller case and buttons. That congealed sweat is up to twenty years old!

• Take apart the optical mouse.

Putting Together

• Fit the circuit board for the mouse into the base of the controller. The mouse board needs to be oriented with the buttons for the mouse on the A and B button end of the controller.

• Note the standouts that need to be removed and use a rotary tool to cut them out.

• Use the razor knife to clean up the cuts made with the rotary tool.

• Use the empty base of the mouse shell to locate the opening for the optical reader.

• Use the rotary tool and blade to cut the proper opening.

• Fit the clear plastic lens and the circuit board into place and make sure everything fits well.

• Test the opening you made and the alignment of the clear plastic piece by plugging the mouse into a computer. Once satisfied that the position is correct, superglue the plastic lens directly to the inside of the base of the controller.

• Place the top of the controller shell on the base and mouse board and determine what parts need to be removed. Use the rotary tool to clear them out.

• You might need to make some additional space for some of the electronic components on the mouse circuit board. Try bending them to fit or you can solder extensions on to some to make more space.

• Put the top in place and use a marker to indicate where the A and B buttons fall on the mouse circuit board. Depending on the space available and where the buttons need to be moved to you may need to remove the old mouse buttons

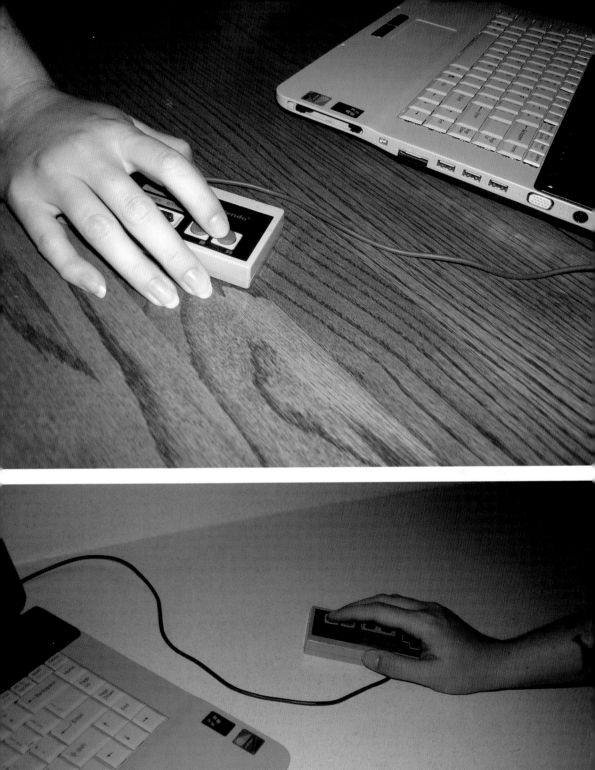

from the circuit board. You will need to move at least one of them. You might need to remove a scroll wheel and the button the wheel activates if pressed. Removing the right and left mouse buttons (Carefully! Don't damage the circuitry!) opens up more space for soldering in the replacement buttons. If careful you might even be able to reuse the buttons from the mouse instead of needing new ones.

• Warm up the hot glue gun and fill the red buttons with hot glue. It's alright to overfill them – you can trim away excess glue with the razor knife later.

• Cut four pieces of wire a few inches long and strip the ends. Solder the wires to the circuit board and button.

• Plug the mouse in again to make sure that all buttons still work properly.

• Use hot glue to position the buttons in the proper places on the circuit board. The B button should serve as the left mouse button.

• Assemble the controller and determine if you need to trim some of the glue off of the backs of the red buttons.

• Depending on the position of the button underneath you may need a bubble of glue extending out or the glue may need to be removed from the inside of the button.

• Reassemble and your modified mouse is ready to use.

Erik Fitzpatrick
MULTIPLE DIGRESSION

Erik Fitzpatrick is a happily married man in full-time employment with a passion for unusual projects that involve electronics. On his website, where he shares his daily musings in a blog, he includes details of some of the more imaginative projects he has completed. These include such bizarre creations as the Intestinal Lampshade, the Remote Control Box and the Humphrey Room inconvenience.

www.multipledigression.com.

'It all started with Rube Goldberg and my mother. As a kid I loved looking at Rube Goldberg contraptions, and started making little contraptions of my own, such as a rope-and-pulley system for feeding my pet hamster without leaving my bed, or a device to raise a flag in our apartment when the mail had been delivered. Over time these creations became a bit more practical than Rube's, but I still love that sense of whimsy. The fact that my mother was a schoolteacher helped teach me the value of making things myself: teachers are notoriously underpaid and thus thrifty, and grade school teachers are constantly stockpiling materials for craft projects.

This typewriter keyboard conversion was the start of my renaissance of making stuff. I've always loved the idea of self-sufficiency and for me the whole craft/DIY/maker ethos is a large part of that. When you make something yourself not only are you saving money and making something you won't find elsewhere, you are also learning techniques that you can apply to future endeavors and thus making yourself a more capable person. I like that.

People now have free time and they want something to do with that time. You can only play video games or watch TV for so long before your brain melts, so why not make something?'

Typewriter Keyboard

Erik Fitzpatrick

Erik devised this modern use for a junk shop find to help his wife find a solution to her repetitive strain injury caused by long hours typing on a computer keyboard. With a little simple wiring, you can use the typewriter to type directly onto your computer screen. Bypass your computer's own keyboard and be original.

MATERIALS

- A computer keyboard
- A vintage typewriter
- Soldering iron
- Adhesive Copper Lamé
- Wire
- Gaffer tape
- Solder
- Silver pen

> Don't be disheartened if you find this project a little tricky to work out – you'll get there! Or you may prefer to try something a little simpler, taking Erik's ideas as inspiration.

INSTRUCTIONS

In a regular computer keyboard, each keypress completes a circuit. There is a little circuit board in there and I mapped all the connections from one terminal to another. This was then replicated inside the typewriter by wires going from the circuit board to strips of adhesive lamé, which contact their counterparts when a key is pressed.

The Basic Keys

• Every time a key is pressed, the 'lever' is pushed down and connects with the 'crossbar' (the other end of the lever raises the hammer to strike the paper). The crossbar keeps the levers from moving too far and provides the force to advance the carriage for the next letter. For this project, each lever and each part of the crossbar that it would contact would have to be electrically insulated. You need something to act as the actual contact. For insulation I used gaffer tape.

• For the contact patches I used copper lamé with an electrically conductive adhesive on the back, soldered in place. After removing the crossbar and covering it with gaffer tape, I replaced it in the typewriter and used a silver glitter pen to mark exactly where each hammer touched it. Then I cut triangular strips of lamé and stuck them on over the contact areas. I used alternating triangles so that each one could have some spot large enough to solder the wire in place – the even ones on one side, odd on the other.

• Next up were the levers themselves. Each lever was wrapped first in gaffer tape then in lamé. Soldering onto this lamé material works, but the problem is that the stuff is so thin that is burns/melts really easily, so any more than a minute touch of the soldering iron would put a hole in it and I would have to start again.

• From here I returned to the crossbar, soldering on wires.

The Special Keys

Enter
• I wanted to be able to hit 'Enter' by slapping the carriage return, so as to reproduce as closely as possible the feeling of actually typing on a typewriter (which you can still do on this thing, by the way – it is still fully functional as a typewriter). What I finally settled on is a mechanism on the carriage itself that is responsible for 'dinging' a bell when the typist reaches the end of a line. There is a small 'hammer' that is pulled right across the 'anvil' when the end of a line is reached. The anvil strikes the bell, shown through the hole in the lower left. After this is done and the end of the line is reached, the carriage comes to rest. When the carriage return is slapped, the hammer moves gently across the anvil, going in the other direction (the hammer is on a spring, so it can pivot counterclockwise around the screw shown).

• Wrap the anvil in gaffer tape and lamé and solder a wire to it. The circuit for 'Enter' is dependant not on two pieces of lamé touching, but on one bit of lamé touching the metal frame itself, in this case the bare hammer.

• Wrap the backside of the hammer in gaffer tape so it won't close the circuit when it rings the bell. Solder a bit of wire to the frame.

• In case there was ever any trouble with this mechanism, I also wired the '¢' key on the typewriter to act as a backup 'Enter'.

Space
• The spacebar was pretty simple, as there was a spot underneath where it struck a rubber pad. All I had to do was make the usual gaffer tape-lamé-wire contacts and it was ready.

Shift
• Basically it was the same sort of contact, but this time wrapped around the bar that the 'Shift Lock' mechanism locks on to. Unfortunately, I had to wrap the locking

mechanism in gaffer tape to prevent a circuit from forming with the frame, and this made it unable to actually lock the shift mechanism around the bar (wrapped in gaffer tape and lamé).

Putting it Back Together

• Solder wires onto the terminals of the circuit board left over from the keyboard. This was a nightmare – each one was maybe two millimeters from the next so getting the solder to stay on just one was a task in itself. Then I found that a few of the wires had lifted the conductor right off the board so I had to scrape off the green insulation a little further up the circuit to redo it (the diagonal one in the illustration), like a junkie looking for a new vein. And half the time fixing one solder job would heat the one next to it enough for it to come loose.

• A few words of advice for anyone trying this themselves: use electronics solder – it doesn't stick to breadboard. I later got curious and tested regular solder on an old NIC and it stuck everywhere. Watch what you buy.

• Like I said earlier, each key is a connection between two terminals. Some terminals have lots of keys connected to them. For example, connecting terminal 4 and terminal 19 might produce 'A' but connecting terminal 9 and terminal 19 might produce 'F'. Since 1-13 always connected to 14-26 and vice versa (ie no terminal from 1 to 13 connects to any other terminal from 1 to 13), I arbitrarily decided that the levers would all connect to 1-13 and the crossbar would connect to 14-26. Next I physically grouped all the wires by terminal, so that everything going to terminal 1 would be bundled together, everything to 2 would be together, etc and labeled the bundles with masking tape and a marker.

• Mark on the underside of the typewriter which lever corresponds to which key.

• With all the wires bundled, it was time to connect them to their corresponding wires from the circuit board. These were crudely soldered and covered with shrink-tubing or, when I forgot to put on the tubing first, more gaffer tape.

• Fortuitously, the circuit board fit nicely in a little space at the back of the typewriter. I made a little insulated nest of gaffer tape and slid it in, where it fit perfectly – nice and snug.

Tom Bugs
BUGBRAND

Tom Bugs works with technology and sound, modifying existing items, such as keyboards and answer phones to make unique sounds. BugBrand builds unique electronic audio devices by hand in Bristol.

www.bugbrand.co.uk

'I've only been doing electronics for three to four years and it's all been picked up off the internet and from books just by constant trying-out of ideas – totally DIY, especially in the extensive use of drills, paints, hardware. I began by circuit bending (short-circuiting electronic kid's toys to make new sounds through malfunction) and making simple guitar stomp-boxes and have just built up from there by experimenting and so today I'm self-employed full-time (and there's never enough time) making these strange devices for musicians all around the world. It's often said that its not what you know, but who you know and I'd say that volunteering at the Cube Cinema in Bristol has certainly helped me out greatly – giving me a bunch of hands-on experience and meeting the constant streams of edge-dwelling musicians who play there.'

Build Your Own Contact Microphone

Tom Bugs

This project shows Tom Bugs's unique vision and will be a must for any musician. No need for expensive equipment. How to build a simple piezo contact mic that can be stuck onto any acoustic instrument or other object to easily get sounds into your amp/mixer/computer.

MATERIALS

• Piezo disc – easily available from electronics stores. Sometimes they come with wires already attached or they are encased in plastic housing and called Piezo buzzers. You can (carefully) hack off the plastic to get the disc inside.
• Mono jack socket – or choose another type of socket if you want
• Two pieces of wire – 8 to 15cm, preferably two different colours (eg red and black)
• Heat shrink tubing (optional)
• Epoxy resin (optional)
• Soldering iron (15 to 25 watts)
• Solder
• Wire cutters

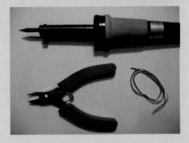

INSTRUCTIONS

Attach wires to Piezo

• Use the wire cutters to strip about 5mm of plastic off the end of each wire. Apply a little solder to the exposed wire (this makes it easier to attach in the next step). Apply a little bit of solder onto the outer metal ring of the piezo and then solder the black wire to this point. Then, quickly and carefully, solder the red wire onto the central disc – this part is fragile and soldering should be done quickly to avoid damaging the disc.

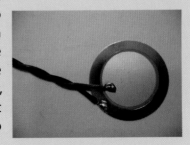

• Twist the two attached wires together to keep them neat and to strengthen them and then add the heat shrink tubing if required (this keeps things even more neat!).

Attach wires to jack socket

• Examine the jack socket and identify which connections to use – the ground connection (the wire attached to the outer metal disc of the piezo) is the one near the hole for the jack plug, and the signal connection (the wire to the central piezo disc) is the connection away from the hole. Strip about 1cm off the ends of the wires and solder them onto the jack plug connections.

Finishing

• To really improve the strength of the contact mic a thin layer of epoxy resin can be added to the top of the piezo – carefully cover the connection points of the two wires as it is these are that the weakest points.

If it doesn't work…

• Check the connection to the central piezo disc – if this has been badly soldered then the disc may have been damaged. You can de-solder the connection and reconnect it (quickly as before!) to another point on the central disc. Some jack sockets have four connection points, two of which become disconnected when a jack is plugged in (generally two connections on either side of the socket) – try connecting the wires to the other side of the socket.

• If you get a lot of hum from the mic (especially when holding it) then the wires may be the wrong way round – check that the ground connection on the socket goes to the outer metal disc and that the signal connection attaches to the inner piezo disc.

I have been considering all the products I use on my skin and hair. I use cleansers, toners, facial scrubs, face masks, day-time moisturizer, night-time moisturizer, eye cream, body moisturizer, hand moisturizer, shower gel, bubble bath, shampoo, conditioner, hair treatments, styling products and sprays but I have no idea what any of them contains. I think carefully about the food I eat but when it comes to the beauty products I use I have no idea about what is used to make them. I am sure that, just as with food, many of the ingredients are preservatives, colorings and perfumes. Those nasty chemical ingredients make the product last as long as possible and look and smell appealing to the customer. Then there is all the packaging that we just throw away and rarely recycle. I started to thinking about how there must be some kind of natural alternative, some other way to clean and moisturize. I am no scientist, I need basic recipes that work just as well. I don't have any specialist equipment, I need simple methods that I can produce at home in small quantities. I don't want factories to be making products that I put on my skin and hair.

So, I have done some investigating to see if there are others who feel the same as me. I have talked to people who are making their own beauty products, their own shampoos, moisturizers and soaps. This chapter contains their recipes, simple step-by-step instructions letting you into the secrets of making your own beauty products. Some contain natural, organic ingredients, others are fun and quirky projects that call for creativity. Whichever you choose to make, you will know exactly what ingredients you are using and the production process will be demystified. Some of them are so simple that you won't ever need to buy them in the shops again.

Gabreial Wyatt
VINTAGE BODY SPA LLC

Gabreial Wyatt's Vintage Body Spa aims to help people create perfect spa treatments in their own home. With emphasis on using natural ingredients, they want their customers to experience a sense of serenity and the feeling of being at a luxurious spa without leaving home.

www.vintagebodyspa.com

'Growing up on a small farm, the outside world was my creative outlet. Making mud pies and leaf salads became a necessity in everyday playtime. The excitement of mixing, mashing and stirring up concoctions for pretend play was where part of my inspiration for Vintage Body Spa came from. Now as a stay-at-home mother, digging in the dirt and getting messy is once again an everyday occurrence in our lives. With my two boys running around there is also a need for "me" time. Not being able to take a trip to the spa as much as I would like, I decided I had to create spa type rituals that I could use on a daily basis. With the growing popularity of natural and organic ingredients my love for crafting products has become a joy to share with my family and friends.

I believe in today's society, crafting has become more than just a hobby. The need to create things with our own two hands has brought us back to those childhood days. As adults we are filling a void of creativity that has become lost in today's fast-paced schedules and routines. Beside the need to unwind and to find those lost creative juices again, crafting has become a way of life for some. With today's mass-produced items, the need for organic, natural and recycled materials has also become a necessity.'

Mental Body Buff (Body Scrub)

Gabreial Wyatt

What better way to start making your own beauty products than with ingredients you probably already have in your own home? Gabreial Wyatt shares with you her recipe for making a body scrub using everyday ingredients.

INGREDIENTS

• 1 cup of Dead Sea salts
• 1 cup of sugar
• 1 cup of organic whole wheat flour
• 1/3 cup of olive oil (you may substitute vegetable oil)
• 2 drops of lemon essential oil or 2 tablespoons of fresh lemon zest

INSTRUCTIONS

• Mix all ingredients thoroughly.

• Apply to dampened skin in a circular motion.

• Buff away dead skin cells and rejuvenate your mood with this skin refreshing Body Buff.

Photography Gabreial Wyatt

Debbie Phillips
GUDONYA

Debbie Phillips runs Gudonya from her home in Wisconsin USA, with an almost fanatical dedication to the production of quality bath and beauty products. Producing a range of lip balm called 'smoothies' in flavours like Vanilla Kiss, Mango and Grape, along with favourites like the Body Kiss exfoliator in Strawberry and Champagne as well as Sweetgrass, Phillips calls on all to indulge themselves with her tempting treats.

www.gudonya.etsy.com

'I am fortunate to have been raised in an artsy environment. My mother is a very talented woman who never set artistic boundaries, but constantly challenged us to dig deeper and not be afraid to try new things. I can remember my mother always making things with her hands, whether it was sewing one of us a new outfit or crafting a new box for my school supplies for my first day of Kindergarten. For me, art is an integral part of who I am and from where I stem. For as long as I can remember, I've loved arts and crafts. Throughout my school years, my never-ending interest in art increased and I attended every class I could. Drawing, stained glass or pottery – it didn't matter. Just as long as I could play. Even now, as an adult with two small children, I am most happy while creating. Memories come flooding back while I watch as my children fashion such fashionable jewelry for me out of foam beads and plastic cording. They beam with pride as they place the necklace of many colors around my neck and say, "We made this just for you, Momma! Do you like it?"

To me, creating is more than just throwing something together for a last-minute gift. It's an imaginative means to create and strengthen bonds between us all. I would not want to be a part of a world without arts and crafts.'

Bath Fizzies

Debbie Phillips

INGREDIENTS

- 2 cups of baking soda
- 1 cup of citric acid
- 0.7oz oil of choice (almond, coconut, shea, etc)
- 0.25 oz fragrance oil
- Witch hazel – 5 sprays

Photography Debbie Phillips

INSTRUCTIONS

• Mix baking soda and citric acid in a bowl. Add the oils and mix. Spray with witch hazel, one spray at a time, until mixture holds together. Don't spray too much or the citric acid will begin to fizz prematurely.

• Fill molds of choice (soap molds or small, empty, washed out food containers work very well), packing mixture in pretty firmly. Allow to dry a few minutes, pop out of mold, then allow to dry for 24 hours. Wrap/package as desired.

SAFETY NOTE: If you do not have access to fragrance oils, essential oils can be used. Keep in mind that although essential oils can provide many healthy/healing benefits, there are many that can be harmful, even in minute amounts, if allowed to come into contact with the human body.

Leah Kramer
CRAFTSTER

Leah Kramer is one of the crafting elite, known by thousands for her work running Craftster – a virtual crafting circle where people meet to talk about their craft projects. Here you can read about anything from how to sew a beautiful handbag to suggestions for craft projects using unwanted CDs. From the wacky to the practical, this craft forum has it all and as a result is a daily visit for many crafters.

www.craftster.org

'It's hard to say where my obsession with crafts came from. I don't come from a particularly artsy or crafty family but I really loved making things when I was a kid. As I got into my teenage years, my interest in crafting diminished a bit because it was really hard to find ideas that inspired me. Then in college I happened to live very close to a craft store and these tiny little glass beads called "seed beads" caught my eye. I quickly fell head-over-heels for making beaded jewelry. It was so soothing to produce beautiful objects by adding one tiny little bead after another. I started selling my jewelry at craft fairs to have a reason to keep making more. In my twenties I stumbled onto a craft fair where I live, in Boston, called the Bazaar Bizarre. At this fair I discovered all of these people who making "crafts" but who were truly cool, hip, irreverent or offbeat. This really refueled my fire to start getting crafty again. The following year I got involved in the Bazaar Bizarre as a vendor and an organizer. Shortly after this I decided to create the website www.craftster.org as a place where people could share ideas with one another that were not just incarnations of traditional, mainstream craft ideas but instead were unique extensions of one's own personality and style and interests. Much to my surprise the website exploded in popularity and at this moment has around 65,000 members with a thousand more joining every month. The website has grown so much that it is now my full-time job to keep it running and I've also written my first craft book called *The Craftster Guide to Nifty, Thrifty and Kitschy Crafts: Fifty Fabulous Projects from the Fifties and Sixties*.'

Quick and Easy Soap Making

By Leah Kramer

In this project, the soap you can make can be transparent or opaque. Opaque soap comes in a nice creamy white color so it's easy to add coloring to make it whatever color you want. If you make transparent soap, coloring can be used to tint the soap. Or instead of adding color, you could make transparent soaps with a small plastic toy embedded in the center of the soap. All these soaps are so simple to make, just melt and pour.

MATERIALS

- Soap mold
- Vaseline
- Big block of clear or opaque melt and pour soap
- Glass measuring cup
- Microwave
- Disposable chopstick
- Liquid soap color (optional)
- Liquid soap fragrance (optional)
- Small spray bottle with rubbing alcohol in it (optional)

INSTRUCTIONS

Choosing a Soap Mold

Soap molds are just made out of slightly flexible plastic. If you're bored with the shapes you see at the craft store, you can go to cake decorating shops and look for fun chocolate molds. They are made of a very similar plastic and work just as well. Between soap molds and chocolate molds and all the stores online that sell them, you can find one in any shape you could ever possibly dream of. Stars, flowers, animals, motorcycles…the variety is unbelievable. Imagine how cool it will be to make custom soaps for friends in shapes they will love!

Preparing the Mold

• Dip your finger in the Vaseline and coat the soap mold in a very thin layer of Vaseline. This just helps the soap pop out of the mold more easily.

• Place the big block of melt and pour soap on a cutting board and cut out small ice-cube-sized chunks and place them in the measuring cup.

• Place the measuring cup into the microwave and heat on high for 30 seconds. This melts the soap into a liquid state. If after 30 seconds your soap is not completely liquid, pop it back in for another 15 seconds. Use the chopstick to stir the soap and to make sure it's totally melted. You can continue to microwave the soap at 15 second intervals until it's completely melted.

• If you'd like to, you can add soap coloring and fragrance at this point. Soap coloring looks a lot like liquid food coloring but it's made especially for soap. Soap fragrance is also liquid and comes in a small bottle. A craft supply store will probably only carry a handful of fragrances but there are endless fragrance choices available online. Just drop a few drops of coloring and fragrance in and stir with the chopstick. Once you become more familiar with soap making you can even add exfoliants like ground coffee, oatmeal, ground apricot pits, etc.

Note: Make sure that whatever you add is deemed safe for use in soap. For example, you can buy safe 'cosmetic grade' or 'skin safe' glitter for adding to your soap but adding traditional craft glitter to soap is not safe.

Pouring Soap into the Mold

• Let the soap cool just a bit. You don't want to pour it into the mold if it's too hot because it can warp the mold. So what you do is stir the soap continually with the chopstick until you notice a very thin skin forming at the top. Then you know it's ready to pour.

• Now carefully pour it into the mold until it reaches the top of the cavity.

• Let the soap cool and harden up. You can put it in the fridge to speed it up but it only takes about one hour to cool at room temperature.

• Now you can pop the soap out of the mold and it's ready to use.

Hannah Elizabeth Howard

LIZZIE SWEET

Lizzie Sweet is a handmade 'bath and body' line inspired by pin-ups, burlesque and responsible living. Started in 2003, Lizzie Sweet strives to show the sexy side of natural, handmade body goodies while inserting a positive image of women of color into our cultural and sexual iconography. Lizzie Sweet Body is run by Hannah Howard, a crafter extraordinaire and founding member of the Department of Craft.

www.departmentofcraft.com
www.lizziesweet.com

'Crafting isn't merely a hobby for me. It's a way of life and a part of my heritage as an African-American. It has been long ingrained in me that working with your hands not only meant you knew the importance of hard work, but that you had a skill no one could take from you – you always had a way to feed you and yours. My aunt Virginia made hats for church ladies to supplement the meager income she made housekeeping as a young woman. My paternal grandmother, Mamie, was a Southern farm girl who quilted not only out of necessity, but as a way to record family history. It's a tradition kept from the time of Slavery when it was illegal for us to read and write and nearly impossible to keep track of family since families were rarely kept intact. Quilts also led the path to freedom for many who braved the Underground Railroad. My maternal grandmother, Hannah, taught me how to cook, passing down her recipes for homemade applesauce, gingerbread and preserving fruit for the winter. My mother taught me to sew and the importance of using your clothes as a mode of self-expression. A child of the 1960s, she made her own clothes in order to stay in vogue, to have the couture fashions her pockets wouldn't allow. I think of these women every time I make something and how their crafting empowered them to make choices during times when choices were limited. Their crafting enabled them to keep family intact, empowered them economically and provided me with something I couldn't buy in a trendy, crafting class.'

Pattycakes: A Solid Skin Smoothie

Hannah Elizabeth Howard

During the winter, Hannah Howard is always fighting to moisturize her skin. She finds that store-bought lotions don't last very long as they're mostly made of water. Pattycakes, little cakes of moisturizer made from natural ingredients, were created as her secret weapon in the battle against ashy skin. Try them and you'll find that your skin is suddenly astoundingly smooth.

INGREDIENTS AND MATERIALS

• 3oz (85.2g) white or yellow beeswax pellets
• 3oz (85.2g) shea butter, coffee butter or mango butter
(you can combine all three, but make sure you're only using 3oz total)
• 3oz (85.2g) cocoa butter
• 3 tablespoons (45ml) virgin coconut oil
• 1 tablespoon (15ml) sweet almond oil
• 1 tablespoon (15ml) avocado oil
• 8 drops essential oil of your choice
(I prefer orange, lemon or peppermint)
• Cosmetic glitter (optional)
• A Pyrex/heat resistant glass bowl or measuring cup
• Microwave or bain-marie (double boiler)
• Measuring spoons
• A rubber spatula
• A plastic soap mold, flex mold, small glass baking dish or candy mold (Note: You can use anything that's heat-resistant and will unmold easily)
• Foil candy wrappers or colored cellophane (optional)

This recipe makes four small pattycakes.

INSTRUCTIONS

• You can prepare pattycakes using a double boiler or a microwave. While the microwave tends to be a quicker method, you run the risk of burning your oils. Use caution and heat only in twenty second increments.

• Combine the beeswax, cocoa butter, shea (or mango) butter, sweet almond and avocado oils in a small glass bowl for microwave or in a bain-marie once the water is boiling.

• Allow all ingredients to melt to clear liquid or microwave in twenty second increments until all is sufficiently melted (it usually takes less than a minute).

• Remove from heat and allow to cool a little before adding the essential oil. You can use fragrance oil, but it's been my experience that essential oils not only have more lasting power, but blend better with the oils.

• If you'd like to add cosmetic glitter for a little skin shimmer, let it cool till it starts to congeal a little and add, stir and pour quickly.

• Pour into molds. Cover molds with plastic wrap and set them somewhere to cool. If you're impatient, you can put them in the freezer or refrigerator until they set completely.

• Once the pattycakes are cool, they should be a solid white or yellow and pop right out of the mold with very little coaxing. If you use a glass baking dish, you can unmold them and cut them into bars. You can then wrap them in plastic wrap and colored cellophane or foil candy wrappers.

• Store in a cool, dry place. Pattycakes have a shelf life of about six months.

Heather Mann
HEATHER JOY

Heather Mann is a self-confessed lip balm addict who loves to experiment with different flavours. Having cracked a foolproof recipe and developed dozens of yummy flavours, she now sells her smoothing creations through Etsy. She explores the new crafting movement through CROQ, a crafty zine of which she is one of the editors.

www.yardenxanthe.etsy.com

'My mother was a huge influence on my craftiness, and both of my grandmothers were quite crafty as well. As I got older, I just took on arts and crafts on my own, without their lead. My sister and I were quite entrepreneurial with our crafting, as well, and we made some nice pocket money as young teens. I also used art and craft in gift-giving to friends and family.

As an adult, crafting has been a way to explore the world and learn more about things that interest me. In lonely times, crafting has been a way for me to connect to the outside world (via websites such as www.craftster.org and www.getcrafty.com) through sharing my crafts and getting feedback on them. Through the internet, I have also been exposed to many different types of crafts that I either never took notice of, or was not even aware of the existence of, to my delight and crafty enrichment.

Before the 20th century, craft was part of life, as most people made a lot more of their everyday objects of daily use, including tools, clothing, etc. People HAD to be crafty, whether they wanted to or not. In recent years, almost none of us have HAD to be creative or crafty, but we have been able to take part in a privilege of craftiness, doing it for leisure, fun and fulfilment. There has been a rise in craftiness because some people aren't happy with the cheapness of mass-market produced stuff. Many people want a way to express themselves. Many want to use and/or give handmade items that have value stemming from the fact that they were not made by a machine and sold by the ten thousand.'

Smooth Cocoa Butter Mint Lip Balm

Heather Mann

This is a luxurious and smooth lip balm that uses a high amount of yummy cocoa butter. Undeodorized cocoa butter will have a slight smell reminiscent of chocolate, and the cocoa powder will further add to the chocolatey goodness. With a touch of peppermint, this lip balm is as delicious as your favorite chocolate mint candy.

INGREDIENTS

- 2 teaspoons cocoa butter
- 2 teaspoons sweet almond oil
- 1 teaspoon beeswax
- 1 teaspoon cocoa powder
- 6-10 drops of peppermint essential oil
- 2 vitamin E capsules
- Sweetener, if desired (stevia or saccharine)

INSTRUCTIONS

- Microwave cocoa butter, beeswax and sweet almond oil in a pourable glass measuring cup for one minute at a time (50% power), stir, and continue to microwave until melted.

- Once mixture is melted, squeeze contents of vitamin E capsules, and add the cocoa powder.

- Mix very well, taking care to fully incorporate cocoa powder.

- Add a very small amount of sweetener at this time, if desired.

- Add 6-10 drops of peppermint essential oil and mix once again.

- Pour into containers. The mixture is enough to make three tubes.

Jamyla Bennu
OYIN HANDMADE

When Jamyla Bennu realized that even some of her favorite 'natural' bodycare items tended to use petroleum, mineral oil, corn oil and other non-nourishing ingredients, she decided she could do just as well by herself and started working on her own recipes. With research, study and the good old trial and error approach, her company Oyin Handmade has striven since its beginning to create products that are not just natural, but nourishing.

www.oyinhandmade.com

'I was raised by very creative parents, and have always known that if there was something you needed, you could probably make it. I learned to sew, knit, crochet, and work with wood during my childhood and have never stopped. The bodycare products I make came out of my inclination to mix, make, and personalize commercial products for my own needs and preferences.

Honey is one of my favorite foods, and also one of the inspirations by which I came to make my line of hair and bodycare products. The name of the goodies, "Oyin", is actually the Yoruba word for honey!

Technology and commerce are booming, and new products are introduced every day. In truth, it can seem a touch overwhelming. I think people are making things in an effort to imprint their personality and individuality on their world; seeking to have a relationship with the objects in their lives other than that of consumer/product.'

Magical Honey Deep Conditioner

Jamyla Bennu

A transformation for your inner kitchen wizard!

Honey is one of nature's most versatile gifts: besides being delicious, it is a humectant (meaning it helps your hair or skin draw moisture from the atmosphere), and a great moisturizer when dissolved in water. It has been used as a natural cosmetic for centuries.

The thing that is 'magical' about this recipe is that it takes ordinary ingredients that many of us have in our kitchens or bathrooms – and transforms any plain drugstore conditioner into a luxurious, moisturizing deep conditioning hair treatment. The recipe is open, leaving you to make the choices concerning which ingredients are best for your hair type and needs. It's great as a monthly protective treat, and can give new life to dry, damaged, over-processed or colored hair.

INGREDIENTS

- ½ cup conditioner of your choice
- 2 tablespoons runny honey
- 1 tablespoon olive, castor or hempseed oil
- Up to 10 drops essential oil (I recommend lavender, tea tree or orange)

INSTRUCTIONS

- Whip ingredients together using a hand whisk or electric beater. Slather onto hair and pin out of the way; let stand for fifteen minutes to an hour. For extra benefit, wrap securely in a warm moist towel. (I generally multi-task, and apply this treatment when I'm doing household chores.) Afterwards, cleanse as usual.

WHICH OIL TO USE?

- Olive oil is high in oleic acid, which gives it a unique ability to penetrate hair and skin; wonderful benefits for shine, softness, and scalp health.

- Castor oil, thick and shiny, attracts moisture to the hair and protects against harsh environmental factors.

• Hempseed oil is a high-fatty-acid oil with a 'dry' feel, that nourishes hair without oiliness.

WHICH ESSENTIAL OIL?
.
• Lavender helps to balance and condition the scalp and is also known for its relaxing, anti-stress benefits. Pleasing floral aroma.

• Tea Tree oil is a natural antifungal, antiseptic, and can be a great help to a problem scalp. Powerful, almost medicinal scent.

• Orange helps to eliminate toxins through the skin, and is also wonderful for its cheerful, juicy scent!

CRAFTY IDEAS

Moisturizing Smoothie Mask

INGREDIENTS
• 1/2 small or 1/4 large banana
• 1/4 avocado (remove the skin and stone)
• One tablespoon of acidophilus plain yogurt

INSTRUCTIONS
• Mash the banana, avocado and yogurt into a smooth paste.
• Cleanse and rinse your face. Do not dry.
• Massage the paste onto your warm damp skin (keep away from your eyes).
• Leave on for ten minutes.
• Rinse off with warm water and pat dry.

Fruity Body Scrub

INGREDIENTS
• 1/4 cup grated lemon peel
• 1/4 cup coarse brown sugar
• One cup grapeseed oil

INSTRUCTIONS
• Mix together all ingredients.
• Gently rub on your body in a circular motion.

Lemon-Aid Face Mask

INGREDIENTS
• One small banana
• One teaspoon of honey
• Eight drops of lemon juice

INSTRUCTIONS
• Mix together all ingredients.
• Apply this face mask after you have washed your face and leave it on for about five to ten minutes.
• Cleanse with warm water and apply toner and moisturizer.

Herbal Mint Facial Toner

INGREDIENTS
• One chamomile tea bag
• One green tea bag
• Two large springs of fresh mint
• Three cups water
• Distilled water

INSTRUCTIONS
• Combine tea bags, mint and water in a saucepan.
• Bring to a boil.
• Mix equal parts of the mixture with distilled water in a spray bottle. (You can keep the mixture in the refrigerator for up to two days.)

Home
Sweet
Home

Domesticity is boring, right? Does the idea of cooking, cleaning, mending your own clothes or decorating your home send a cold shiver down your spine and cause a feeling of dread to grow in your belly? Not for a new generation of people who are beginning to embrace the lost skills of previous generations of women and use them to transform their homes and their lives. A few years ago, I would have thought it ridiculous if someone told me that I would soon enjoy learning long forgotten domestic skills – that I would be contemplating sewing my first patchwork quilt or knitting my own hats and scarves. I would have laughed if I had been told that my friends and I, more used to hanging out in sweaty clubs watching noisy guitar bands, would be starting craft circles, making our own clothes and baking bread and cakes by the dozen. I don't know when the idea first struck me that domesticity was cool, that it was fine to care about these things. I don't even think it's about growing up, about getting older; people of all ages are beginning to celebrate the cult of the craft.

I have slowly become obsessed with domestic life. I buy vintage kitchenware on Ebay. I sew tablecloths on my sewing machine. I hunt continually for the perfect dinner plates. I almost drool over baking ware. I stalk the ideal sized cupcake tins. I love small and sometimes useless kitchen gadgets. I admit it, I collect vintage teacups. I want to build my own furniture. I own a fully stocked toolbox and power tools.

I am not sure when this domestic obsession started, probably when I first left home at nineteen. I realized that I wasn't prepared. A friend and I shopped for cutlery, crockery, glasses saucepans, baking trays... The list was endless. It seemed that we needed to prepare ourselves for adult life by collecting all the necessary props. I didn't realize that I hadn't yet really mastered the basics of cooking and once leaving home, living in cramped student accommodation, that I probably didn't need the domestic items I had amassed and they would sit gathering dust in the grubby shared kitchen. But it was my first step to domestic life and I have slowly learned to adapt it to my needs. I have realized that that is the secret – you need to make it work for yourself.

The Quiet Revolution

Jean Railla was the first of our new craft generation to celebrate 'New Domesticity', using the phrase to describe a conscious and deliberate form of domesticity. She has described her own route to claiming a domestic life, one which echoed the lives of many other women in the city. Living on her own at twenty-eight in a rented apartment in New York City with a busy work and social life, she felt that this lifestyle was neither satisfying nor sustainable. She realized that as a self-declared feminist, she had been consciously rejecting anything she at that point reduced to the label of 'women's work'. However, as she became aware of this rejection, her approach altered: 'I began re-evaluating who I was and what I wanted, including many of the things that I had always dismissed because I didn't want to be one of "those" women. Were cooking, crafts and keeping house something that would limit my life? I had always thought so, but living like a slob wasn't very enjoyable. What did I really have to fear from domestic entrapment?' She began to rediscover the crafts she enjoyed in her childhood, knitting, sewing and cooking, realising that this fun could be transferred to adult life. Jean's discovery was that this not only improved her surroundings but it could also be really enjoyable.

This isn't about settling down and making a cosy little home for yourself. Domestic does not equal dull. Countless young women in their twenties are returning to domesticity with a conscious sense of feminist history. Looking after yourself and your home has long been dismissed as an unsatisfying and thankless task. But why can't taking care of yourself, your surroundings, your family and your friends be rewarding? Such work has long been devalued, with the implication that it causes more frustration than fulfilment. It is not the activities themselves that are limiting but how they are viewed, as 'simple' and somehow stifling. But these perceptions are misleading, when craft and domesticity can be creative, artistic and rewarding – an artistic expression of everyday life. Your hand knitted jumper, as practical as it may be, can be a work of art – and the same goes for your newly decorated one-bedroom flat or your kitchen.

This isn't about emulating Martha Stewart or Nigella Lawson or about trying to be a perfect wife or mother, far from it. The movement holds strong ties in punk rock 'Do-It-Yourself' communities, stemming in part from the Riot Grrl underground movement of the early 1990s where women challenged the male dominance of the music scene. It is a distinct part of an independent cultural ethos set apart from the commercial world, a resourceful way to live your life, a way to personalize your own environment. *Bust* magazine editor and influential author of craft book *Stitch 'n Bitch*, Debbie Stoller proclaims that 'crafting is the new rock 'n' roll'. And it does feel like a new form of rebellion. It can be a radical move to take out your knitting on the bus. Your actions may be dismissed as a simple form of a passive women's hobby but you are showing that you just don't care about all those old outdated preconceptions. Besides, it is not just women who are embracing the new domesticity; men are also taking an active role, challenging stereotypes of their own. For many people, celebrating the domestic is about forming a sense of wider community. Previously, embracing domesticity would mean embracing a devotion to your home and accepting a certain amount of isolation that this would bring. Contemporary crafters do not follow this stale and limited vision, and instead meet up to discuss their work in groups, over dinner or drinks at the bar. It is a way to connect with others, to share forgotten skills and of course provides a perfect cover for gossip.

Many online forums have sprung up celebrating the new domestic arts and people are joining in their thousands. For example, the website www.craftster.org has 55,722 members regularly posting information about their current craft projects and countless more logging on to just take a look and find inspiration. Their motto? 'No Tea Cozies Without Irony.' No one could criticize these crafters for not being creative, for just reliving a nostalgic sense of building a perfect but unimaginative home. Here people are often working on a tight budget, there are students, people experiencing the optimistic excitement and mild sense of disappointment of moving into a shabby rented flat, young newly weds and single mothers. All share the common aim of transforming the place they live into their home, and in doing so they recycle old materials, customize a thrift store find and reuse supposed 'junk' they find abandoned in the street, always working to express their creativity across their walls. The unexpected thrives: you often get the best results from the

most limited resources. Browsing through Craftster, I am so often amazed by what people are up to – from decorating their living rooms and creating beautiful furniture from ugly shabby finds to making quilts from old T-shirts and customizing old lamps into works of art.

This new found love for the domestic doesn't have to take over your life. It's about being able to make choices and deciding what best suits you. I can't cook but I can bake up a storm, I am not a knitting expert but I love to embroider. Even if you only ever just knit one scarf, sew one baby blanket, decorate one room, you'll feel great – there's a real sense of achievement and empowerment through craft. There are no rules, no expectations, just be yourself, find your crafty side and have fun.

Have I convinced you yet? And before you start to panic – imagining ugly ornaments or dodgy tea-cosies – rest assured you won't find any cheesy crafts in this new domestic movement. This chapter is dedicated to the domestic side of the new craft movement. It is about feeling proud of your home and yourself.

Julie Jackson
SUBVERSIVE CROSS STITCH

There are so many preconceptions about embroidery. The image of the still, silent figure working at a domestic craft has been repeated countlessly in paintings and novels. The new wave of 20th century crafters are breaking apart this stereotype and none more so than Julie Jackson.

www.subversivecrossstitch.com

'I did some cross stitch back when I was a pre-teen, mostly because we went out to the country every weekend to see my grandparents and there wasn't much for a bored kid to do out there. Since then, I've never been a hardcore crafter, but I'm always looking for some form of art therapy. My mother always said that when I was a little girl and I wanted something, like a new purse, I would make it. In grad school, I made a six-foot papier maché monster, which was really great therapy. So I do a little bit of everything, whatever's fun and as long as it's enjoyable.

In fact, Subversive came about because I was stuck in a horrible job with an idiot boss and I needed a way to channel my frustration. I was wandering through a craft store one day during my lunch break and everything was much sweeter than I happened to be feeling, so I picked up some intricate flowery designs and decided to change the sentiments by changing the words. Some of my co-workers started giving me ideas for phrases, and I started putting them online just for kicks. I think it helped us all make it through the day.

I think that taking up a craft makes time slow down, and may be the closest thing to meditation or quiet time that a lot of people get. It's something that's incompatible with multi-tasking, and it brings you back into your own physicality and allows you true creative space. And afterwards you have something tangible to show for it. Even if you follow a pattern, your interpretation of that pattern is absolutely individual.'

Is That All There Is?

Julie Jackson

Julie Jackson creates detailed samplers, a form of needlework traditionally used by young girls to practice their sewing techniques. But whereas traditional samplers feature carefully stitched alphabets, family trees or passages from the bible, Jackson's samplers brazenly display her outspoken attitudes. Her samplers aren't framed sentimentality, they are subversive messages. I first saw her work in magazines a couple of years ago and was surprized to see samplers exclaiming messages such as 'Babies Suck', 'Bitch', 'Irony is Not Dead' and 'Kiss My Ass'. Her samplers are a form of active self-expression, she subverts all preconceptions of the passive crafter. To explain her crafty intentions, Jackson pointed me in the direction of Rozsika Parker's book, *The Subversive Stitch* and her ideas about the traditional expectations and the subversive nature of crafting. I had never considered that needlework could be such a radical act, a secretive cover for women to express themselves. The image of a sewing woman, silent and working on a homely task is not always what it seems.

MATERIALS

• Cross stitch fabric: If you use 14-count, this will easily fit in a 4" x 6" or 5" x 7" frame (the final measurement will be 4" x 6").
• Needle: size 24
• Embroidery floss: Pick whatever colors you like, or use these (you will only need one little skein/pack of each color). DMC brand colors: Black/310, Red/606, Yellow/307 and Green/320.
• Hoop: Get one that's about 5" round, or close to that
• Embroidery Frame
• Pres-On Mounting Board (optional)

INSTRUCTIONS

Preparing

• Grab some scissors and keep them handy. Cut a piece of the fabric – about 12 x 10" roughly – enough to hang outside of the hoop when it's clamped tight. You can always make it smaller later. Also, the edges may fray a bit but don't worry about that.

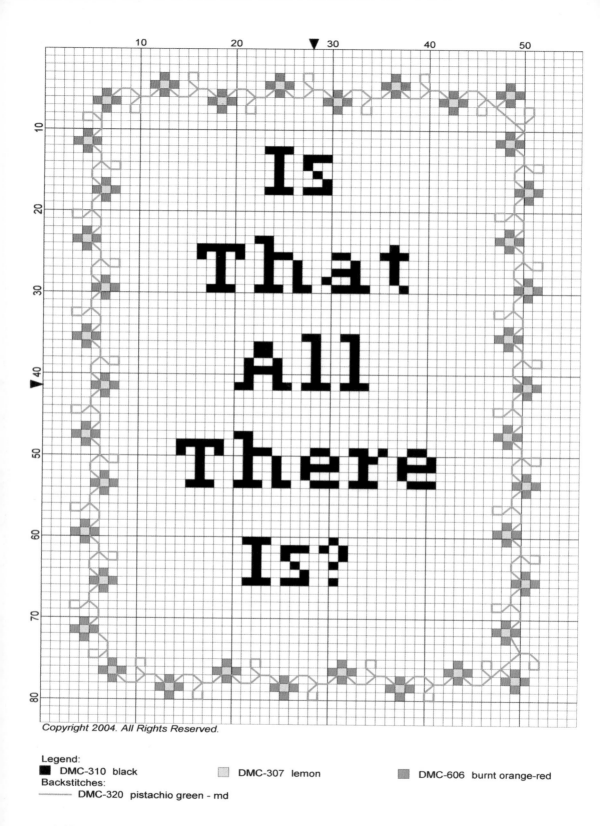

Is That All There Is?

Legend:
■ DMC-310 black   ▨ DMC-307 lemon   ▧ DMC-606 burnt orange-red
Backstitches:
— DMC-320 pistachio green - md

• Put the fabric in the hoop. Basically, you want it to look like the top of a drum: put fabric on top of the small part of the hoop, then snap the larger part of the hoop over the whole thing. You'll have to loosen the larger hoop to do this, but once it's there, make sure it's as tight as you can get it.

• Separate the embroidery strands – you'll see that what looks like one string is actually six smaller strands. You will use only two strands at a time.

Begin Sewing

• Find the approximate center of the pattern. Then, find the approximate center of your fabric.

• Begin stitching something that's near the center of the pattern. Working this way (from the center out) will ensure that you don't stitch right off the material. Start with the word 'All' and go from there. Then you'll just count spaces from there and follow the pattern.

Stitching

• This pattern is very simple and almost always requires only the basic 'X' stitch. This one also requires a straight stitch – also called a backstitch.

•To begin cross stitching, bring the threaded needle up from the back of the fabric leaving about a one inch tail of thread behind the fabric.

• Stitch the next five or six stitches over the tail. Clip off extra thread.

• To end, weave your needle back through the last 5 or 6 stitches and clip the thread short so as not to leave a loose tail.

Stitching Tips

There are two methods. The first method is to work a row of half stitches (////), then work back (\\\\) to complete the 'X's. Use this method for most stitching. The second method is to complete each X as you go. Use this method for vertical rows of stitches. The main thing is that each 'X' crosses in the same direction. That is, the top thread of the 'X' should always slant in the same direction (either \ or /). It doesn't matter which way they slant, but if they're mixed the finished piece will look uneven. The straight stitches are done just exactly how they look – no 'X's required. Be sure to relax as you stitch. Your stitches should lie flat on the fabric and not distort it. Check out the animated stitching on the on the 'How-To' page of www.subversivecrossstitch.com – this will show you exactly how to do it.

Changing Colors

• Sometimes a color will have only a few stitches and then 'jump' to another area. Most of the time you should end off and start again, other times you can carry the thread along the back. Be aware that sometimes the thread will show through the white fabric.

Finishing

• It's a good idea to wash the finished piece if you have time, but if it's clean you don't have to. If you do, just hand wash it in some cold water with Woolite or very diluted detergent.

• Let it dry fully, then press with an iron. If it scorches, it will wash out. A scorch looks like a light burn. Like toast.

To finish

• To frame, use a standard-size frame, like 5" x 7", that comes with a hard cardboard insert.

• Center the finished piece on the cardboard and sew in big zigzags on the back so that the fabric is taut on the front. You can also use tape and just tape the edges to the back of the board. Or buy a package of Pres-On Self-Stick Mounting Board.

Secret Quilting

Even as recently as a hundred years ago, women in America were using quilt-making to express their political and social views. Making patchwork covers for beds in the family home often wasn't just about keeping their family, or the family they worked for, warm. Just because they expected to work in the domestic realm didn't mean that their views were silenced. If sewing is your activity then it can also be your outlet. Before women were given the right to vote, their needlework often expressed their opinions. I was fascinated when I learned about this. It seemed surprising, but it makes sense. I know that the patterns used in American quilts were often meaningful and the images depicted details of their communities and recorded family events but I didn't realize that they were also a political act carried out by women with little other opportunity to express their views. I started to pore through books on the subject, eager to learn more about the use of quilts to tell stories and truths in their stitches. There are many myths that African American slaves used a quilt code to navigate the Underground Railroad. Quilts with patterns appear to have contained secret messages that helped direct slaves to freedom. A plantation seamstress would sew a sampler quilt containing different quilt patterns. The image of a monkey wrench sewn onto the quilt would mean that the slaves should prepare the practical, mental and spiritual tools they would need from a long journey. A picture of a wagon wheel would instruct slaves to board the wagon to begin their escape. Flying geese would point out the direction they should follow to find their freedom.

But quilt historians and Underground Railroad experts have questioned whether these claims are accurate, whether there is any truth in the stories. The theory is that slaves would use the sampler to memorize the code. The seamstress then sewed ten quilts; each composed of one of the code's patterns. The seamstress would hang the quilts in full view, one at a time, allowing the slaves to reinforce their memory of the pattern and its associated meaning. When slaves made their escape, they used their memory of the quilts as a mnemonic device to guide them safely along their journey. Unfortunately, there is no evidence to prove that the specifics of this theory are true, no quilts remain and it hasn't been documented in any oral accounts, but this at least illustrates the potential of the quilt as a means to transmit hidden messages. What is certainly true is that women of the abolitionist movement in America's North against slavery made quilts illustrating their beliefs. They held craft fairs to raise money for their cause and to generate publicity. The first was held in Boston in 1834, and it was so successful the idea spread to other cities and towns throughout New England, and then to other states such as Ohio and Pennsylvania.

It is fascinating to realize that the sewing skills that many women now reject as oppressive and limiting were once one of the only forms of power that many women possessed. Reading about a group of women in Willamina, Oregon, who in 1915 stitched together a quilt, known as 'The Murder Quilt', to raise funds for the defense of a woman accused of murdering her husband made me realize how so many women found their voices through the act of sewing. It is a shame that quiltmaking continues to be dismissed by many as a simple domestic task.

For from being just a domestic act, quilting can be a form of artistic expression. Gee's Bend is a rural African-American community based in Wilcox, Alabama, where a tradition of highly improvizational quilting has existed for generations and has become famed, and exhibited in galleries across the country. Far from using a rigid pattern, the quilters explored every conceivable variation on the form. Most striking is a section called 'My Way', which contains the most improvizational 'no holds barred' quilts in the exhibition. 'My Way' is the term used by the quilters to describe the pieces that come from their own individual styles. The Gee's Bend quilters used whatever fabric scraps were at hand, generally preferring to use them in long strips, fitting them together like a puzzle as they went along, rather than laying out rigid patterns. The color combinations and fabric choices are stunning. The quilts are made from any fabrics they could find, often denim, corduroy, upholstery, formalwear and prints are combined in the same quilts.

Denyse Schmidt

Renowned American quilter Denyse Schmidt, works in a similar way, breaking the rules of quiltmaking. Her quilts are huge splashes of color, twisting shapes in bold fabrics. They are quite different – contemporary takes on the traditional quilt. Previously, I had been put off quiltmaking when the patterns I saw in books weren't what I could see fitting into my own home. However, Denyse Schmidt's quilts are the kind of quilts that I want to be making, beautiful, detailed works of art.

'My parents were both skilled craftspeople. They both had full time careers, but my mother made most of the clothes for us kids and herself, and my father made furniture and did a lot of work around the house. Nothing they made ever looked crafty or homemade – they were very skilled, and the aesthetic was of the time (early 1960s), very clean and modern. I think I took it for granted that if you needed something you just made it, and it was usually of better quality than you could buy. It took a while before I realized that not everyone made things.

While I dislike making generalizations, these kinds of trends are cyclical, and we are ripe for a new movement of craft/DIY/handmade. The web has been an interesting component of the current trend, and I really like how folks are sharing their work on a global scale – a kind of cyber sewing circle. Our lives today are so saturated with technology and our attention spans fragmented by the blitz of information that comes at us every moment – the process of making with our hands is a good antidote to this. It is tactile, and gratifying, immediate (rather than virtual).'

Mix-It-Up Cocktail Coasters

Denyse Schmidt

Stitched up in colors reminiscent of your favorite cocktails – frozen margaritas, blue lagoons, mint juleps and martinis with a twist – these coasters make a perfect gift. Give them away, along with a set of coordinating swizzle sticks or glasses.

Select six fabrics in shades of lemon and lime; then layer them three to a pile, and cut out the pattern pieces. After that, shuffle the pieces to mix up the colors and see what you get!

Makes six coasters, finished size: 4" square

MATERIALS

FABRIC

For Coaster Backs
Lime green solid: about 1/8 yd.

For Coaster Fronts
Total of about ¼ yd of cotton fabric pieces, scraps or remnants, comprising the following (or your favorite) colors, each cut into 5" x 8" rectangles:

'Lemon Yellow' plaid
'Cocktail Shaker Silver' geometric print
'Curaçao Blue' solid
'Crème de Menthe Green' solid
'Olive Green' solid
'Lime Green' solid

OTHER MATERIALS

Cotton batting:
About 1/8 yd

INSTRUCTIONS

• From Lime Green, cut 4 ½" squares for Coaster Backs. From cotton batting, cut six 4 ½" squares for Coaster padding. Set aside.

• Stack three Coaster Front fabric rectangles (any three of six colors), right sides up, with edges aligned. Lay out the pattern pieces on top of fabric stack, and pin through all the layers (FIGURE 1). Cut out all the pieces. Repeat with remaining three Coaster Front fabric rectangles.

• Position each color separately as shown in FIGURE 2.

• Create unique color combinations for each coaster by shuffling fabric pieces until each block has mix fabrics and colors. You can work systematically, moving all A pieces around first, for instance, then moving B pieces, and so on. Or you can improvise, swapping colors until you're pleased with results (FIGURES 3 and 4).

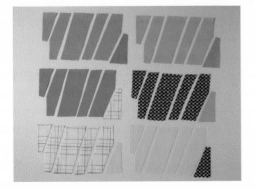

Figure 1

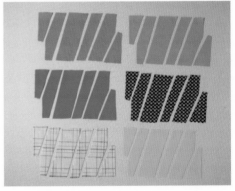

Figure 2

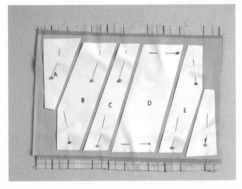

Figure 3

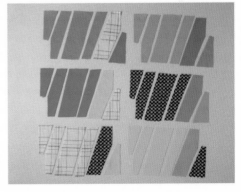

Figure 4

• Stitch all Coaster Front pieces together, aligning points where seam lines intersect on each piece (FIGURE 5). Press seam allowances of A and F pieces toward their outside edges. Rest of seam allowances should be pressed toward darker fabric. Square up each Coaster Front to 4½ " square: then machine-baste around perimeter of each one, 1/8" from edge (FIGURE 6).

• Center one square of batting on wrong side of each Coaster Back, and machine-baste around perimeter of each one, 1/8" from edge.

• With right sides together, lay Coaster Fronts on Coaster Backs, aligning edges and pinning if necessary. Leaving ¼" wide opening at center bottom for turning, stitch around perimeter of square, pivoting at corners. Backstitch at beginning and end of seam of secure stitches. Trim corners.

• Turn each coaster right side out through opening. Use point turner to push out corners. Press flat. Slipstitch to close opening, or machine-stitch close to edge of folds.

• Stitch-in-the-ditch* to quilt Coasters, or machine-quilt if you prefer.

*To quilt this stitch, stitch very close to the seam line, on the side without the seam allowance directly underneath.

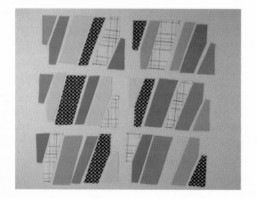

Figure 5

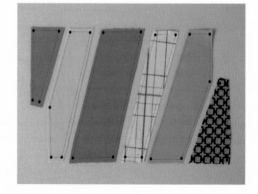

Figure 6

Mary Lyvers
MY HOUSE IS CUTER THAN YOURS

My House Is Cuter Than Yours is a collection of domestic undertakings; including crafty endeavors, thrifty finds and delightful dishes all with vintage appeal. A member of girl gang the Dixie Dolls, Mary Lyvers' crafty beliefs and values centre around 'being able to turn a horrid discarded item into a lovely hostess gift that will be the envy of the party!' The central aesthetic here is reinvention: reusing and recycling unwanted items with just a little imagination.

www.myhouseiscuterthanyours.blogspot.com

'I got crafty by means of necessity. I wanted to gussy up my house in my own style, along with giving my friends nifty gifts but I had limited cash and faced even more limited resources. There just wasn't anything out on the market that seemed to be the right gift for "thanks for making me that yummy vegan chocolate cherry cake" or "happy birthday you skank, I love your trashy ass". I get most of my crafting influence from mid-century culture and styles. I like crafts that have a bit of an edge to them but are also heavily inspired by the perfect appearance and sometimes odd imagery in sources such as vintage magazines and books on decorating, cooking and hobbies. Most of my crafts start out either as something picked up at a thrift store or stuff that would generally be discarded, also know as scrap craft. I then alter, repurpose and recycle these thrift store finds or scraps into some vision of loveliness that I hope to be the envy of the cool kids. My current crafting happenings involve getting together with my crafty girl gang, the Dixie Dolls. We enjoy crafting, cocktails and trash talking and are also the hosts of an annual bizarre holiday bazaar. This is held at our local independent record shop, East Hill CD. Entertainment is provided by television horror hosts Nightmare Theatre, with a drive-in movie style showing of a festive holiday film such as the 1960 Mexican cult classic *Santa Claus*. We Dolls sell our "perfect for the gift giving season" wares and trinkets, which are primarily made from recycled items turned into funky housewares and fashion accessories.'

Scrap Craft Vintage Style Notepads

Mary Lyvers

These little notebooks are a quick and easy craft project. They are ideal for grocery lists and to-do lists and are a cute vintage style addition to your kitchen.

MATERIALS

• Food packaging boxes that have a look to them that you like
• Paper
• Stapler
• Ruler
• Scissors (regular and pinking)
• Optional embellishments eg decorative papers, stamps, stickers, ribbon, interesting candy wrappers

INSTRUCTIONS

• Cut out front and back of the box including about an inch of the top flaps as well.

• Measure and cut out pages slightly smaller than the covers. Don't make more pages than your stapler can handle though.

• Crease the extra inch of the top box flaps over and towards the non decorative side of your covers. Start construction by laying down front cover flat face up on work surface. Next center and place down the top (smidgen less than an inch) of the stack of paper overlapping just the flap section of the cover not concealing the decorative front. Next place back cover of notebook face down matching it up with the front cover. Staple through just the flaps and the stack of paper, not through the to-be-seen part of front and back covers. Smash down sharp points of staples if needed. Fold covers back into place.

• Disguise the stapled flaps and boring blank inside cardboard with paper cut to size.

• Cut edges of paper with pinking shears for a decorative look.

Heidi Kenney
MY PAPER CRANE

Heidi Kenney of My Paper Crane makes all sort of weird and wonderful creations for the home, including everything from plush vegetables, plants and even toilets! The one unifying theme is colour – all items are bright and bold. You'll be surprised to find little eyes and smiling faces in the most unusual places! Above all the emphasis in on having fun.

www.mypapercrane.com

'The first time I tried origami, I was making a paper crane. When I was finished I was so amazed that a simple square of paper could be turned into something so beautiful! The name My Paper Crane tries to embody that thought, the idea of taking something simple (whether it be fabric, paper, etc) and turning it into something amazing.

Like anything else you might love, I make time for My Paper Crane because I love creating things. I think it also helps that I do not watch television either (unless you count Netflix!).

Because I'm pretty busy I rarely take custom requests. When I try and make something that is not my own idea, its hard to get excited about it. My heart has to be into it! However, if you have something you really have your heart set on, send me an email and we might be able to work something out.'

Cupcake Pot Holder

Heidi Kenney

MATERIALS

- Patterned fabric
- Pinking shears
- Heat protectant fabric
- Sewing machine
- Bias tape
- Pom pom
- Fabric glue
- Felt circles (for eyes) in black and white

INSTRUCTIONS

• Cut out one of each of the pattern pieces (see over – scale up to required size using a photocopier) and pin them wrong sides of the matching fabrics.

• Cut out all the pot holder pieces. You can use pinking shears to help keep the fabric from fraying.

• First layer the heat protectant behind the bottom half of the top cupcake.

• Using a tight zigzag stitch sew down the cupcake bottom to create the lines on the wrapper.

• Using the same stitch lay the top frosting part of the cupcake in place and use the stitching to sew it around the scalloped edges that cover the bottom wrapper fabric.

• Next align the cupcake back fabric so it matches up with the rest of the sandwiched cupcake, pin it in place.

• Take your bias tape (which you can buy all readymade in many different fabrics) or you can create out of any fabric using a bias tape maker sold for a few dollars at most craft stores.

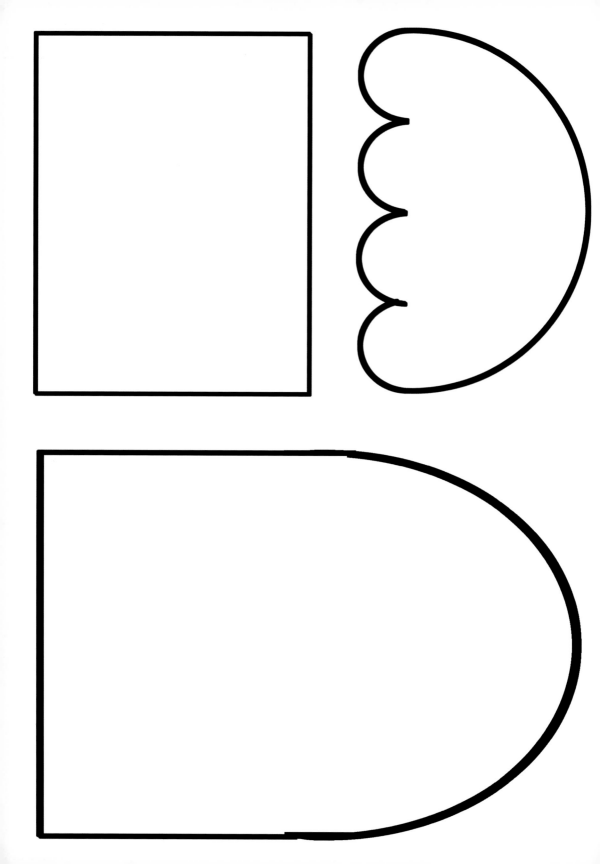

• Pin the bias tape in place all the way around your cupcake. Pin it only to front side of the cake since this is the part you will machine sew first.

• With the cupcake face down sew the bias tape the whole way around removing your pins as you go.

• Next you have the back side of the bias tape to sew, this you will want to do by hand. Using a whip stitch in a thread that blends into your fabric stitch the bias tape in place the whole way around. When you get to the top of your cupcake you can create a loop of the bias tape and tack it into place with a few strong stitches. This will make your potholder loop so you can hang it.

• Next take a sparkly pom pom and hand sew it in place over the bottom of the looped bias tape.

• Using red embroidery floss stitch a small smile onto the front of the cupcake. You can hide your end knots by putting your needle in where the eyes will go. Once your smile is done glue the eyes on using a heavy fabric glue, over the thread knots.

• Let the eyes dry over night before using your potholder!

Wendy Aracich
CIRCLE CIRCLE DOT DOT

Wendy Aracich is a twenty-six-year-old mother who still dreams of the days when she was a child herself. Not because life was simpler then, she says she is happier than she's ever been. It's the clothes that she misses – the pink pinafore dresses with ruffled underwear beneath, the awesome white tights with the soft red polka dots. Circle Circle Dot Dot has been created as a means for Wendy to share her love of all things 'girly' with others. She makes accessories and clothing to sell on-line, and housewares to brighten any interior.

www.circlecircledotdot.com

'I still dream of my favorite girlhood clothes. It's an intense nostalgia that leaves me wishing that I were still cute and small enough to pull them off. It's this love of all things cute and little girly that has influenced my crafting. I'm drawn to fabrics that remind me of those clothes, stitching them into accessories, handbags, housewares and gifts for the grown-up girl who is still nostalgic of her childhood days. I want my goods to be fun, carefree, and ultimately to make the owner happy and bring some "handmade cuteness" to her life.

What else...besides a love of all things cute? I'm a mother to the world's sweetest little boy with the blondest hair and the bluest eyes. I live in North Carolina with my husband, son, and our cat Jasper, who tries to lend a hand with the sewing but just doesn't seem to understand that he can't operate a sewing machine. When I'm not sitting amongst piles of sewing or rifling through stacks of fabric at thrift shops and fabric stores, I'm carrying around a sketchbook and dreaming up more product ideas than I'll ever be able to create...'

Cherry Oven Mitt

Wendy Aracich

Make Wendy's adorable kitchen accessory and wear your oven mitts with pride. You can use your own fabric selections, choose your own decorations and never be burned by hot pots again.

MATERIALS

- Fabric remnants in three different patterns
- Batting
- 5/8" wide ribbon
- ½" wide double-fold bias tape
- Embroidery floss
- Thread

INSTRUCTIONS

- Enlarge pattern pieces (page 187) OR cut four rectangles from newspaper, freezer paper or another lightweight paper in the following dimensions (HxW):

(A) 4 x 7"   (B) 4.5 x 7"
(C) 3.5 x 7"   (D) 10 x 7"

- If making your own pattern pieces, place a bowl or other rounded object with a 7" diameter or more at the top of pattern piece D. Trace to create a rounded top to the pattern.

Cut the following
A: cut 1, B: cut 1, C: cut 1
D: cut 1 back piece (same fabric as A), 2 lining (same fabric as C), and 4 batting

- Align the top of C with the bottom of B, wrong sides together, and stitch. Align the top of B with the bottom of A, wrong sides together, and stitch. Trim seams.

- Pin pattern piece D to finished front and cut out shape so that it matches the other pieces.

185

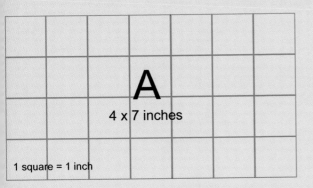

A

4 x 7 inches

1 square = 1 inch

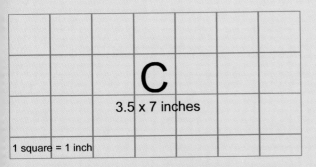

B

4.5 x 7 inches

1 square = 1 inch

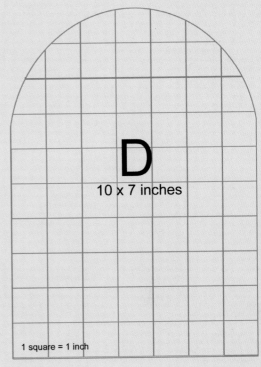

D

10 x 7 inches

1 square = 1 inch

C

3.5 x 7 inches

1 square = 1 inch

• Cut three pieces of ribbon in the following lengths: 1½", 2", and 1½". Align each piece with bottom of oven mitt front, left of center, about ½" apart and pin.

• Embroider around all four edges of each ribbon using pink embroidery floss and a running stitch.

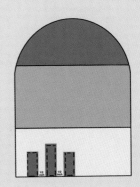

• Pin fabric together in the following order from bottom to top: lining fabric (right side down), 2 pieces of batting, oven mitt back (right side up), oven mitt front (right side down), 2 pieces of batting, lining (right side up).

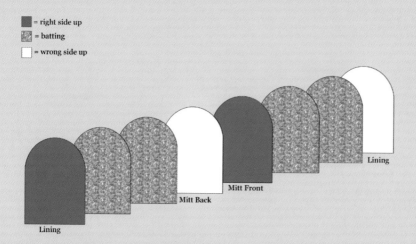

■ = right side up
▨ = batting
☐ = wrong side up

Lining

Mitt Front

Mitt Back

Lining

• Stitch around three sides, leaving bottom edge open. Trim seams.

• Turn right side out.

• Pin and stitch bias tape to bottom edge, following package directions. Leave a 6" 'tail' to fold under and stitch to create a loop near the left seam.

Variations

Play around with the fabrics, colors and trim for a completely different look. For an even simpler project, use a solid piece of fabric for the front and back.

Angela Spencer

My mother, Angela, is the one who first encouraged me to sew and taught me the crafty basics. So who better to ask to contribute a project for this book? She hadn't crafted for years, I think work and family got in the way, but she is slowly starting again.

'Raising a family after the Second World War, my mother had to make all our clothes by hand. So she spent her evenings sewing little suits for my brother, dresses for me with knitted shawls and cardigans and dungarees for us both to wear while playing in the garden.

At thirteen, in the early 1960s, I was learning to sew and knit at school. At home, I was crafting too – making Christmas presents for the family, maybe an apron or embroidered pot holder for my aunts or a storage box covered in fabric for my uncles. My mother had an electric sewing machine and I used it whenever I could, mostly I made clothes. I liked the 'French look' whilst all the other girls were looking like Olivia Newton John in *Grease*. I made A-line skirts and dark sweaters and thought I was the height of French sophistication.

In the later 1960s, life was easy for the crafter. Short shift dresses were simple to make – just two side seams with a zip at the back. The early 1970s bought a craft revival. I learnt how to spin wool and dye it with natural dyes before knitting it into very itchy sweaters. I learnt to crochet and make baby blankets and ponchos from wool and little bags and cushion covers from cotton.

When my children were babies, in the 1980s, I made them smocked dresses and knitted blankets, jackets and little socks. I enjoyed working together with other women at our fundraising craft circles. We took the children along too and the little ones who were interested could begin to learn too.

Amy is now encouraging me to craft again. Maybe one day soon, I will start one of my retirement projects – four old chairs up in the loft that need renovating and recovering.'

Crocheted Slippers

Angela Spencer

MATERIALS

• Two 500g balls of Double Knit cotton or similar yarn
• Small amount of contrasting colour yarn if wanted for trim
• Crochet hook size 5mm
• Two 10cm pieces of any contrasting yarn as stitch markers

STITCHES

Chain (ch)
Double Crochet (dc)
Decrease stitch (dec)
Slip stitch (sl st)

SIZE

The pattern size is for slipper of 24cm length. The size may be increased by increasing the number of rows in the foot section.

INSTRUCTIONS

The slippers are worked in one piece; they are worked in rounds for the toe section, then rows for the foot section.

Toe Section

• Round one. Make 4ch, join to first ch made with sl st to make a circle.
• Round two. Make 6dc into circle.
• Round three. Place a piece of the contrasting colour yarn around hook to act as marker for first st of 2dc into each of 6dc (12st).
• Round four. Place stitch marker at the first st of each round.* 1dc into next st, 2dc into next st.
• Repeat five times to end of round (18st).
• Round five. Marking first st with marker, 1dc into each of 18st.
• Round six *3dc into next st, 2dc into next st, repeat * 3 three times, 2dc (22st).
• Round seven. 1dc into each of 22 st.
• Round eight. *3dc into next st, 2dc into next st, repeat * 4 four times, 2dc (27st).
• Round nine. 1dc into each of 27st.
• Round ten. *3dc into next st, 2dc into next st repeat * 5 five times, 3dc (33st).
• Continue in rounds and working in dc until work measures 10cm.

Foot Section

• Turn work, 1ch, (to count as first st of row, so mark st with marker) misses next dc. 1dc into each of next 22 st (23st).
• Continue working in rows making 1ch as the first st of each row; miss next dc 1dc to end (23 st). Until work measures 23cm from start, or adjust for larger foot size.

Shape Heel

• Row one. 1ch (first st of row) 8dc, dec 3 stitches, 8dc (20st).
• Row two 1ch, 6dc, dec 3 st, 7dc (17st).
• Fasten off work leaving long end of yarn.

Finishing Off

• Sew heel edges together on wrong side of work, using long end of yarn.
• With same or contrasting colour yarn and starting at heel, work 1dc around top edge of slipper.
• Make another slipper to complete the pair.

Betsy Greer
CRAFTIVISM

Betsy Greer is an asker of questions and a maker of many things. Combining these traits she runs the politically-minded craft site, Craftivism, based on the premise that activism + craft = craftivism (for more on craftivism see page 228). For Betsy, crafting is more than a passing fad or child's play or a backlash to early 1990s Riot Grrl politics. As she states on her site, 'Craft is a way of rejoicing, passing time, meditating, harnessing power, sharing and keeping creative forces in motion.' Crafter culture operates as both a community building tool and a means of peaceful protest.

www.craftivism.com

'I honestly can't even remember ever seeing anyone knitting ever, unless it was on television, and even then it was your stereotypical grandmother. I was surprized when suddenly in 2000 I got the itch to learn. In 2000, knitters were very much in the closet. When I asked at the beginning of a weekly staff meeting at the New York City publishing house I worked in if anyone knew anything about knitting, everyone but two people in the room raised their hand. Much to everyone's surprize, no one knew the others knit. It was one of those bizarre moments where everyone looked perplexed and somewhat sheepish, saying, "You too? Really?" One of them had a friend who was in a knitting circle, and passed along her email address. It was at one of those meetings that I learned to knit and have been forever thankful for that opportunity. It's incredible how many women who grew up in the 1970s-1980s like me, did various crafts at a young age but abandoned them to play sports and do other things opposite to the domestic. During those years, if anyone would have suggested we take up knitting, I'm sure we would have scoffed. Because we wanted to be where the boys were, showing them that we, too, could be tough and strong and didn't belong in the kitchen. But somehow enough distance passed between our tomboy youths and we realized that there was value and strength in knowing how to throw a football and darn a sock. And that the domestic was not something to mock, but something to wholeheartedly embrace.'

Crafty Rugs

Betsy Greer

The first thing you need to do for either of these two rug-making projects is to make a peg loom.

PEG LOOM MATERIALS

- Wooden dowels
- Hand drill
- 2" x 4" piece of wood
- Tape
- Hand saw
- Pencil and ruler

Peg loom pictured: Maggie Regendanz
(www.corkwoodonline.com)

PEG LOOM INSTRUCTIONS

- Take 2" x 4", mark off evenly where you would like dowels to go on top of wood, should be evenly spaced with about ¼"– ½" in between holes once drilled.

- Once you have marked holes, take a pen or ice pick and nick a tiny divot in the wood for the drill bit to find easily and hit (this prevents drilling error).

- Wrap small piece of tape around drill bit (that corresponds to dowel width) as a guide for the bit.

- Drill holes for dowels in wood, checking every few holes that the tape doesn't slide.

- If using a long dowel rod, cut shorter dowels, one for each hole, each about 4" long.

- Once completed, turn 2" x 4" over and using hand saw, create a cradle for the dowel to rest in.

- Drill holes in dowels small enough for the twine to pass through, using cradle to keep dowel from rolling.

- Once finished, sand rough edges on dowels and loom if desired. Woodwork accomplished, get to weaving!

T-shirt Rug

MATERIALS

• Peg loom
• Old clothes, rags, towels, linens
• Cotton yarn and twine
• Yarn needle
• Fabric scissors

INSTRUCTIONS

• Thread twine through dowels, approximately 2.5 times the length of the finished piece, tying knots at the end.

• Cut fabric into long strips about 1" to 2" wide

• With fabric pre-cut, weave in and out of pegs, when you reach end of strips, backtrack a few pegs to secure fabric in weave. (Alternatively, tie a knot, which will create a bump, but will ensure fabric won't come loose.) The woven fabric is called the weft.

• Continue weaving in and out of the pegs until dowel is almost full, then pick up each dowel individually and slide woven fabric down the warp (the cotton twine). Make sure warp is lying flat on the floor or table at first so you don't lose the woven fabric!

• Repeat until you have woven desired length, leaving a few inches at the top.

• Cut warp from dowels and tie fabric securing warp to weft.

Fleece Rug

MATERIALS

• Sheep's fleece (the longer staple the better, approx 3lb)
• Bath towel
• Water source with hot and cold taps
• Liquid dish detergent
• Bed sheet
• Felting needle (optional)

INSTRUCTIONS

• Lie bed sheet as fully open as possible on floor, then lie bath towel on top.

• Using bath towel as a template for size, spread out wool in horizontal/vertical layers.*

• Wool has tiny hooks in the fiber that connect when pulled or twisted (like in spinning) or when put in hot water the fiber locks and becomes felt.

• Keep stacking the layers horizontally and vertically until 2-3" high.

• Take sheet and fold over fleece and bath towel, so you have a sheet and fleece sandwich.

• Carefully take bath towel to the water source and place inside. (You could use a bath tub.)

• Squirt liquid detergent over fleece.

• Cover fleece entirely in hot water.

• Now the fun part, stomp on the fleece for about five minutes in order to compact the fiber. (Don't be alarmed if the water turns brown as sheep are outdoor creatures and get muddy.)

• Drain water and repeat filling up the water source, stomping with cold water for five more minutes.

• Drain and roll the now wet and soggy fleece and towel sandwich lengthwise and stomp for five more minutes.

• Unroll and repeat steps above from the hot water. (At this point, the fleece should be compacted into a felt rug.)

• Lay flat to dry.

• Once dried, any holes or weak spots can be corrected with extra fleece and a felting needle.

Notes
*Depending on the condition of the wool, you might need to tease out the fibers beforehand. Wool with a short staple isn't best suited for this type of project as it won't felt correctly. Some wool may need to be rinsed out at first if it is exceptionally dirty, in order to layer.

Janet McCaffrey
PRIMROSE DESIGN

Primrose Design was started by Janet McCaffrey as a part-time business in 2003, and was created to combine her lifelong love of design with the needlework skills learnt from her grandmother. Specializing in one-of-a-kind pillows and accessories handcrafted from vintage linens, fabrics, buttons and trims, McCaffrey's designs involve bright colors in unusual combinations and indulge her love of mixing patterns – plaids with polkadots, stripes with graphic florals.

www.primrosedesign.com

'I've done crafts for as long as I can remember. As a child I loved to draw and make collages from magazines and throughout high school I took as many art classes as I could and then majored in graphic design in college.

After a series of increasingly uncreative jobs and positions that took me away from the actual designing and into management, I found my way back to crafts by making pillows and selling them to friends, and that planted the seed that maybe I really could make crafting work. I left my full-time job and started freelancing, officially started Primrose Design, and began selling on consignment to local shops. The website and online shop soon followed. And I became part of the online community of crafters through sites like Craftster and the Switchboards, making contacts with like-minded crafters all over the world.

Most of my current projects involve fabrics and sewing. I'd been collecting vintage fabrics, embroidery and quilts since college so already had a good start on the collection of materials that now form the basis of my work. And I still spend a lot of time at the weekends roaming around flea markets, garage and yard sales, and antique malls looking for new materials to work with. You can find wonderful (and inexpensive) treasures if you keep your eyes open to their possibilities. Vintage curtains and tablecloths are perfect sources of fabric for pillows or purses. Vintage dinner napkins, tea towels and handkerchiefs make wonderful pillows, sachets, and smaller items. Look for old buttons, beads, ribbons, and millinery trims, too – all make interesting additions to your projects.'

Recycled Vintage Handkerchief Pillow

Janet McCaffrey

MATERIALS

• Vintage handkerchief
• Cotton fabrics: small piece for the center, about 1/8 yard for the inner border and about ½ yard for the outer border and back
• Four vintage (or new) buttons
• 18" x 18" polyfil or feather pillow insert

INSTRUCTIONS

• Choose a vintage handkerchief that you like and cut it into quarters. If the handkerchief wasn't quite square to start with, make sure each quarter is exactly the same size.

• Cut an 11" square of coordinating fabric and lay the handkerchief pieces over it with the points facing the center. I've left some space between the pieces for this pillow, but you could position them closer together so they meet in the center.

• Pin the layers to hold them while you sew the buttons onto the points. Choose pretty or funky vintage buttons depending on the style you're going for. You could also use one large spectacular button if your points meet in the center – when you sew the button make sure you catch all four handkerchief corners with the thread.

• Now for the borders. Cut two strips of fabric 2" x 11" (I used scraps from another project), and sew them onto opposite sides of the 11" square, using a ½" seam allowance. Press the seams to one side. Cut two more strips 2" x 13" and sew them to the remaining sides. Press the seams to one side. Do the same thing for the outer borders, using two strips of a second fabric that are 4" x 13" and two that are 4" x 18" to make a finished piece that is 18" x 18". Set the top aside while you make the back.

• This pillow has a simple envelope-style back. To make it, cut two pieces of fabric 13" x 18". I used more of the black and white polkadot, but you could use a completely different fabric – or two. On one long side of each piece, turn up ½" of fabric and press. Turn up ½" again and press. Topstitch along the folded edge.

• To put the pillow together, lay the top face up on your work surface. Lay one of the back pieces face down with the topstitched edge in the center, aligning at the top. Place the second back piece face down on top of the first, aligning along the bottom. The back pieces should overlap in the center by at least 4".

• To prevent dog-eared corners on the finished pillow you'll need to taper the corners. Mark points ½" in from the corners towards the center and 3" away from the corner along each side. Draw lines from these points and trim away the extra fabric. Pin all the pieces together so they don't slide around while you're sewing them.

• Sew all around the outside edge using a ½" seam. Turn the right-side out and press the seams open. Slip your pillow insert inside, making sure it doesn't bunch up anywhere and that it fills out the corners. And you're done!

• Using this basic pattern you can make a pillow in whatever size you like. Change the width of your borders, add another one, or make a larger pillow. If you have tiny scraps of fabric to work with, make a patchwork border. Add rickrack, some ribbons, or more buttons. Use your imagination to come up with your own unique design.

Knitting in Public

When I was a little girl my mother took me to a market in Hong Kong with endless stalls of brightly colored wools and ribbons, brilliant fabrics hanging overhead and baskets of needles covering tables. Everything a crafter could ever want was on display and all around sellers were calling out to you, urging you to buy. Whenever we had been to this market before, I was always dazzled by the colors of the materials laid out in front of me, and begged for a length of ribbon or a handful of shiny buttons without having any idea what to do with them. I think my mother thought it was time I learned to knit and decided that day that she would teach me, just as her mother had once taught her. She let me pick needles (pink) and a ball of wool (pink, again) from the masses of wools. I remember feeling overwhelmed with the choices. I had entered a secret adult world. This seemed different from my drawing or play dough creations. This was a secret craft, there was a technique that needed to be learnt. I remember trying, ambitiously, to turn my little ball of wool into a pair of legwarmers. Once I had mastered the knit stitch I must have thought they would magically appear. I soon gave up in frustration, throwing down my needles. My little hands would not quite work together in the steady rhythm that knitters soon develop. Since then, over the years, many people have patiently tried to teach me my forgotten basics. But I am impatient, I want to rush ahead and create. I still have little patience for techniques or patterns.

About five years ago, I had the urge to knit again. I had read about people like me, women in their twenties who wanted to reclaim the skills of the handmade for their feminist generation. I was intrigued. I bought some more needles and chose some fancy wool and asked my mother to try again to teach me to knit.

I have to admit that I will never be the world's greatest knitter. I tend to knit a few rows, examine them carefully, criticize my own uneven stitches and then unravel it and start again. I have unraveled so many more stitches than I have ever kept on my needles. It has taken hours of concentration for me to get the hang of it and I still worry that I am on the verge of forgetting everything. A friend of mine claims that there is what she calls a moment of 'Knitting Epiphany'. When you start to knit, it won't make sense. You won't be able to get it right. It will be all knots and dropped stitches then suddenly, almost magically, it will make sense. Suddenly you will be able to knit. You might be doing something entirely different. You might be asleep, walking down the street, at work or eating dinner and suddenly you'll know how to knit. You will have had your knitting epiphany. The next time you pick up your needles you will be able to knit. You'll still need practice but the basic understanding will be there. At first it seemed to me like trying to knit was just trying to tie knots with sticks. I suppose that's all it is really. But once you get the hang of the looping and twisting you can make anything. That amazes me every time I pick up my needles. This is the secret that holds it all together.

I have to be honest, knitting is addictive. Something about the satisfaction of finishing a row will make you want to finish the next row and then the next before you put your knitting down. You won't want to stop as you see what you are knitting take shape in your hands. Your addiction will be fuelled by the beautiful wools, textures and colors. This is a tactile art, slow and steady. It is about championing the handmade. It doesn't matter what you knit, how misshapen your hat is when you've finished knitting it, or how uneven the sleeve lengths are on your hand-knitted jumper, it's how you make it that's important and the fact that you made it yourself.

Shannon Okey
KNITGRRL

Shannon Okey is a crafting whirlwind. She is the Cleveland city coordinator for indie craft fair Bazaar Bizarre (see page 35) and manages several crafty and creative online shops and communities, below.

www.knitgrrl.com
www.anezkahandmade.com
www.anezkamedia.com
www.fiberleague.com
www.shannon-okey.com

'I'm from a family of artists; my parents even met in art school. To be honest, I was always a little jealous of my mother's ability to paint, it's something I wish I could do as well as she can. Embroidery appealed to me first – it gave me a chance to use my sense of color and composition in a different medium. When I first learned to knit, it was fascinating how fluid knitting was compared to needlework, and when I learned to spin, the possibilities expanded exponentially. Having total control over the yarn is probably my favorite thing about spinning. What I want more than anything is to see more people take on the crafter mindset in their daily lives.

The difference between a handmade item and its discount-store equivalent is multifaceted; the latter is made of lesser-quality materials, may be produced under inhumane sweatshop conditions, and has no "soul". When I wear something handknit, I know that each stitch was made by a person – someone who cared enough to tuck in the ends properly, who put thought and effort into making a beautiful item, who took pleasure in both the creation and the end result. I know that each dropped stitch or mistake makes my piece one of a kind, and that no one else on earth has something just like it. In food terms, no grocery store tomato will ever taste like the one you grew in the backyard!'

Red Light District Peekaboo Scarf

Shannon Okey

Shannon Okey has taught countless people to knit with her *Knitgrrl* book series. Her aim is to make the craft appeal to a new, young knitting audience with her own appealing knitting projects. She has devised a unique project for this book – a scarf with a cheeky twist. This scarf provides an opportunity for the wearer to give viewers an up-close-and-personal inspection of its contents. The photographs (this project uses naughty naked knitter photos from the 1950s) can't be seen clearly unless the 'window' running down the centre of the scarf is picked up and held away from the back. Like a locket filled with secret treasures, this scarf can be used to hide a photo of your beloved, a picture, a poem – anything you choose.

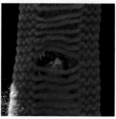

The Provisional Cast-on

To begin this project, you will need to use a provisional cast-on. A provisional cast-on is simply a temporary cast-on, which you can later remove. The chained cast-on uses a knitting needle and a crochet hook of equal size. For a provisional cast-on, do the cast-on row using a piece of spare yarn in a contrasting color (so that you will easily be able to see the cast-on stitches when you come to remove them).

• Make a slip knot, and place it on the crochet hook.

• Holding the crochet hook in your right hand, place it over the knitting needle that you hold in your left hand.

• Hold the working yarn under the knitting needle and yarn over the crochet hook.

• Crochet a chain stitch by pulling the yarn held within the crochet hook through the loop on the hook.

• Move the working yarn back under the knitting needle and yarn over the crochet hook.

• Repeat this until the desired number of stitches have been cast-on.

• Cut the yarn and pass the tail through the loop on the crochet hook to tie off. You can tie a knot in the end of this tail to identify it later as the side of the cast-on from which to remove the chain.

MATERIALS

• One skein (or less) of yarn of your choice, approx 150 yds (can be shorter or longer if you like). Shown here: hand-dyed worsted wool by Shannon Okey.
• Knitting needles of the appropriate size. Used, for yarn shown here, US #8 (5 mm). Can be flat or circular.
• Cotton fabric, paper-backed fabric sheets or iron-on inkjet printing sheets and fabric of your choice.

INSTRUCTIONS

There are two methods for approaching this scarf, depending on your preferences. It can be knit in the round, as shown here, with the 'peekaboo' photos inserted inside the tube. Or, if knit flat, the photos can be printed directly on a larger piece of fabric which can then be used to back the scarf. Directions follow for both techniques.

Circular (resulting scarf is 3-4" wide)

• Using a provisional cast-on, place 22 stitches onto short circular needles or 3-4 double pointed needles.

• Place marker and join round, being careful not to twist. Knit until scarf is desired length or you run out of yarn.

Straight (resulting scarf is 6-8" wide unless you cast-on fewer stitches)

• Using a provisional cast-on, place 22 stitches on your needles.

• Knit until scarf is desired length or you run out of yarn.

Next, for both methods

• Do not cast off yet. In the center of the scarf (stitches 11 and 12), unravel these stitches back to the beginning of the scarf. A wide 'ladder' of yarn strips will result. Don't worry – it won't unravel further as long as you keep the rest of the stitches on your needles while picking them apart. If your yarn sticks together a bit, you can use another needle, crochet hook or even the blunt tip of a tapestry needle to unpick them.

• Once you're almost back at the beginning, cast off the stitches at the end of your scarf. Then, unpick the final few stitches, take out your provisional cast-on, and cast off the stitches at the beginning. You now have either a tube or a flat scarf with a wide ladder of unraveled stitches in the middle.

Making the Peekaboo

• Print the photo of your choice onto fabric. Craft stores carry a number of options, from paper-backed fabric sheets to iron-on inkjet printing sheets.

• If you make the smaller, circular version of this scarf, paper-backed fabric sheets are easiest to use – just run them through your inkjet printer like a regular piece of paper and cut out the shapes. Or, if you iron a paper-sized piece of cotton quilting fabric very flat, it can often be put through an inkjet printer as-is.

• However, if you knit the flat version of this scarf, you'll have a much wider surface to cover. I recommend cutting a piece of fabric the length and width of your scarf and ironing on the motifs before stitching the fabric to the front piece.

• If you prefer, you may turn the scarf inside out before inserting the images. You can also, instead of binding off the stitches all at once, decrease every other stitch until you have a pointed end and add a tassel.

Removing the Provisional Cast-On

• Starting at the side of the chain with the knot tied in the tail, pass the end of the tail back out through the loop that secures the end of the chain.

• Pulling the loose tail carefully, unravel the provisional cast-on's crochet chain one loop at a time. As each knit stitch comes loose, place it on a knitting needle, being careful not to twist your stitches. Bind off.

Tsia Carson
SUPERNATURALE

SuperNaturale is an independent site dedicated to Do-It-Yourself culture in all its forms. From simple afternoon home improvement projects to radical lifestyle choices – the creators of SuperNaturale love them all. They celebrate ingenuity, creativity and the handmade through articles and advice written by passionate crafters.

www.supernaturale.com

'I come from the art side of the field – that being my background and training – along with a lot of "extreme" crafters that I know. I think many of us got fed up with the limitations of art, and its context, and ended up being more interested in our everyday lives. I think that people wanted to make things that have immediacy, usefulness and intimacy. And then what we started doing looked more like craft. But is it craft? I mostly identify myself as a "maker" to get around the great and meaningless divide between art and craft. I see myself and the other people editing SuperNaturale moving away from being object oriented and moving towards less definable, more lifestyle-oriented "crafts" – like grease cars, permaculture, guerrilla green spaces. Although I continue to see actual objects that blow me away.

Understanding why so many people are crafting is complex. I was asked about the rise in popularity of craft by the press after 9/11. Frankly, this offended me as they were fishing for a certain answer – one that had to do with people wanting to retreat to their homes. In fact, this trend had been clearly rising well before the tragedy in the US. It is no coincidence that those of us raised in the "golden" craft age of the 1970s re-embraced and re-popularized the trend once we had some control on media culture.

At craft's radical fringes, the places I like the best, it's popularity is a rejection of consumer culture and a search for spirituality and community in the handiwork.'

Super Chunky Tunisian Crochet Scarf

Tsia Carson

MATERIALS

• A broomstick (or you could use a piece of dowel of the same size).
• 60 cm (2 yds) of jersey fabric – tissue weight preferred. You can use wool, cotton or even recycle and felt old sweaters (see page 87 for more on felting). Make sure that the fabric that you choose won't fray. Be warned, this is a materials-intensive project. You always use more fabric than you expect so make sure you buy or collect extra.

INSTRUCTIONS

Making the Yarn

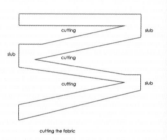

cutting the fabric

• Take your fabric and cut it into one continuous strip about 6cm wide. Accuracy is not that important – you just want it to be roughly the same width. This is the most time consuming step, taking perhaps forty-five minutes to an hour.

Crocheting the Scarf

This scarf was made with Tunisian crochet – a beautiful technique where the front side of your work looks woven and the backside is purled just like in knitting. People believe it to be the ancient proto-stitch to both crochet and knitting. However, you can easily substitute regular double crochet to create it. In Tunisian crochet you do not turn your work, but instead work into your initial row from right to left, in what is called a forward row, and then return from left to right, essentially casting off, in what is known as a return row.

First Row

• Make a slip knot.

• Create the foundation chain of 46 stitches (the final two chains are your 'turning' chains). Do this with your hands by pulling the loops through using your thumb, fore and middle fingers like a pincer. This is a good way of getting the gauge.

Second Row

• This is your forward row. In this row, you are going to put all your new stitches on your broomstick or dowel. Begin with the second chain stitch of your foundation chain. Pull your yarn through the front chain stitch of your foundation chain making a loop. Put this loop on your broomstick. Repeat this technique for every stitch.

Third Row

• This is your return row. In this row you are going to cast off all the stitches you just made. Begin by making a loop around your broomstick and pulling the loop closest to you over your new loop.

• Repeat again, this will give you the correct height for the row.

• Now make a loop over your broomstick and pull two loops off.

• Repeat for the row until there is only one loop on the broomstick.

• Push another loop through this final one so you have the right height for the next forward row.

Fourth Row

• In this row the project gets a little tricky. Instead of creating loops that go through the front loop of the previous row we are going to put a loop through the front vertical part of the stitch known as the front vertical bar. This is actually easier to see than the front chain.

• Begin with the second vertical bar. Pull a loop through each of these and put it on your broomstick.

Fifth-Seventh Rows

• Repeat your return rows as you did in the third row but continue to crochet your forward rows as you did on the fourth row.

• Bind off and weave in your ends as you normally would with crochet.

This technique could be easily applied to make throws and rugs. For a looser gauge, you can make the scarf without using the broomstick but instead cast the stitches on and off your forearm, using your whole right hand and arm as a crochet hook.

The Knitting Resurgence

Knitting has become so popular in recent years, it seems like everyone is learning to knit – or relearning their early knitting lessons. It makes me incredibly happy that I have people to knit with. It is so much more enjoyable to knit in the company of other knitters (even though if I start chatting I do tend to forget that I'm knitting, drop a few stitches, then it's time to unravel my rows and start again).

I never knew that knitting could mean so much – after all, it is only wool and sticks. For many, it's a quick and easy escape to a much more simple time, vital for some during this fast-paced, often tiring age. It's a way to interact with others, slowing down and communicating on a simple level, away from the technology that aims to make interactions quicker, but in reality causes us to miss out on more personal everyday contact.

Knitters are initiating conversations, sociable strangers are asking what they are doing and the uninitiated are asking to be taught how to knit. This 'knitting in public' has become a recognized activity amongst crafters, a deliberate reclamation of the craft from stale preconceptions.

For some, it might appear strange to see young women or teenage boys knitting in public. But this is a new, unabashed movement, and the idea is that knitters in public can indulge in an activity they love while at the same time promoting it to others. Anyone can take part.

Knitting is no longer seen just as a hobby to engage in behind closed doors, it is an activity that a whole new group of people are turning into social resistance, a playful act of crafty rebellion. It is now being used as a guerilla protest, as a political act that challenges capitalism and consumerism on a global scale. No longer a passive and non-radical activity or a dull pastime for the politically unaware, knitting is finding a new and subversive role. People are meeting at knitting groups and ideas are being generated just as fast as the stitches are knitted. When people meet, chat and put the world to rights, anything can happen.

Freddie Robins's knitted wedding, organised by Cast-Off.
Photography Angus Leadley Brown

Stitch 'n Bitch

Today's urban crafters are not interested in working on their projects in isolation when there is so much more fun to be had by creating in the company of friends. The current wave of new knitting groups began simply enough. Debbie Stoller, the editor of American new-wave feminist magazine *Bust* wanted to share her love of knitting with her friends. After spending a three-day train journey from her home in New York to Portland, Oregon knitting, the perfect name sprang to mind: Stitch 'n' Bitch. This wasn't going to be some old fashioned knitting circle, this was something new. This was a chance for New York urbanities to meet and work together on a stress-free hobby. The name summed up their attitude, bringing crafting into their everyday lives and having fun.

And the idea caught on. Soon Stitch 'n' Bitch groups were started all over America, in cafes and bars and even in their members' living rooms. It spread from Chicago to Texas, Utah to Seattle and beyond to Britain, China, Australia, Israel and everywhere in between.

Stitch 'n' Pitch

It is not just women taking part; growing numbers of men are joining knitting groups. They are often encouraged to help break gender stereotypes concerning who is a knitter. On July 28, 2005, the Seattle Mariners hosted 'Stitch 'n' Pitch Night' at Safeco Field. More than 1,600 baseball fans, both men and women, brought their knitting needles and balls of yarn to the game. It was organized by the National Needlecraft Association as a way to promote knitting and it worked. In the 2006 season, twelve Major League baseball teams will hold Stitch 'n' Pitch events across the country. It has proved to a great success – attacking stereotypes while having fun.

Worldwide Knit in Public Day

Danielle Landes noticed that some people were too shy to knit in public, worried about the reactions of strangers. She decided to do something about it and organized a Worldwide Knit in Public Day.

'I used to frequent a knitting forum where there was a discussion about knitting in public. Some of the knitters said that they would never be able to work up courage to knit in public. So I came up with this idea to help them feel more at ease knitting in public. People seem to be more willing to try new things if they know that other people are also trying them. I think it's important to help people feel more confident in themselves, and if this helps, then that's great. Something else that's happened with wwkip day is that people are meeting other local knitters and making new friends who have the same interests. I think it's important to put aside all other differences and find a common interest with someone else. It helps break down barriers that people have, so that they can become friends. It sounds corny, but I really think that if more people could do this peace would be more of a reality, and I think wwkip day helps accomplish that.

In 2005, the first year; there were several hundred participants. This year there were around 6,000 that I know of. That doesn't include all of the people who knit on their own, that's just the gatherings. I think this event will continue to grow each year as more people learn about it. This year we only had two months of preparation, for 2007's events we'll have a full year of planning behind us.'

Cast Off Knitting Club for Boys and Girls

Contemporary crafters who choose to knit in public are consciously challenging preconceptions. These outings aren't just surrealist fun or a form of artistic expression. They aim to introduce knitting to a cross-section of people, taking craft to the people and in the process creating new fans, finding like-minded recruits and turning them into devoted knitters. In their aim to share knitting with others, no one is excluded from the club. It grows steadily and at each meeting more people join.

Knitting is no longer seen as some geeky hobby to work on alone once you get home from work, but can be a visible part of your everyday life. As Rachael Matthews, founder of the Cast Off Knitting Club, who is interested in the craft's public aspects, points out: 'It seemed odd that you were allowed to read a book on the tube, but knitting was abnormal.' It seems that the act of knitting addresses the need to connect with others in an anonymous and often hostile public space. I have also found that when I take my own knitting out in public people become interested, often asking if I will teach them to knit. For some, it must seem like a magic trick that they want to know the secret to. Knitting breaks down barriers, it makes a situation instantly non-threatening. On the tube, people will stop trying to avoid each other's gaze and watch interestedly as you knit. Knitting in public has risen in visibility and may have been adopted by the 'hip crowd' recently, but people have always knitted together, as a way to create and share stories and the details of everyday life.

Cast Off leaflets
© Rachael Matthews and Amy Plant

Rachael Matthews
CAST OFF

Rachael Matthews appreciates the potential of knitting as a contemporary and creative pastime. In 2000, she co-founded the Cast Off knitting club. This London club organized a variety of activities as an alternative to the traditional craft networks. Their meetings are as far removed as possible from the traditional image of crafting. With an adventurous spirit, they organize meetings in unexpected public places. They bring knitting to the tube, to the park, even to London's exclusive Savoy Hotel.

www.castoff.info

'I can't remember how I got crafty. I started making things out of mud and bottle tops and moved onto looking for old net curtains and tights, in an attempt to look like I was in a dance troop on "Top of the Pops". I grew up in a wood in the Lake District, and my grandparents lived next door. There was only my brother and I in the wood, so I made my friends on the sewing machine, and my Grandmother helped me make a school for us all. Every Christmas and birthday my parents would give me a new tool or craft kit, so as I grew up my skills grew. I'm still learning skills. Craft is a way of life and everything I make defines the era it was made in.

When I think about the rise in popularity of craft I like to imagine how these skills first emerged... Once upon a time we were apes and we had little thumbs and then our thumbs grew so we started to twiddle them, which made us feel anxious. Then we learned that by using our new thumbs we could pick up pencils, scissors, knitting needles and crochet hooks. We started to make things and realised that not only were we decorating our homes, and each other, but we were also making inner worlds where we found love for colour, materials, and while we worked we found space for our senses, reflections and prayer. We need to practice our craft skills to prove we are human.'

How to Knit a King Fish

Rachael Matthews

This pattern is made up of written instructions and charts. The charts are to guide you and as no two fish are the same, you are not expected to follow them exactly! The important thing is to follow the overall shape by increasing and decreasing. The colour work is basically three stripes in flower garden, rose and white, with black spots placed in an organic, all over spotty pattern. There is a pink purl stripe, running up the side of the fish. Most fish seem to have one! Let this stripe be the middle, and have fun knitting your fish scales around this.

MATERIALS

• 1 pair 5mm needles
• Lion wool – 1 ball of each. col. 099 winter white, col.140 rose, col.153 ebony, col.202 flower garden.

ABBREVIATIONS

k=knit, p=purl, rep=repeat, st=stitch, tog=together, inc=increase, dec=decrease, patt=pattern.

INSTRUCTIONS

TAIL, FRONT
• Tail has two fins, one big, one small, both in two colour rib.
Make one side of tail in two parts following chart. Put tog on one needle.
• Next row. P2tog in black all along the row until last st. k1 =11sts.
• Next row. K2tog in black, * k1 white, k1 black, rep from * to last 2 sts, k2tog in black.
• Make the other side of the tail in the same way, but put the big and little fin the other way round.
• Now work on body as follows

BODY
• Follow chart. The body is knitted in intarsia. There is a vertical line of purl stitches that run down the length of the fish. Use this as a central marker when following the chart.
• When you reach gills, knit two lines of cable in black. To make the eye, make white bobble, by inc 3 sts into 1 st, then work 3 rows over those 3 sts in garter st. Dec by lifting 2 sts over the first st. Continue in patt to end of row. Stitch French knot onto eye in black.

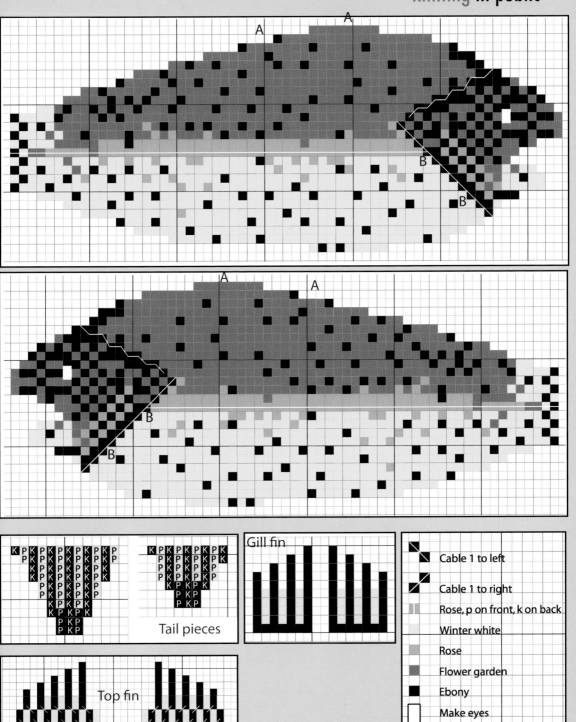

Tail pieces

Gill fin

Top fin

	Cable 1 to left
	Cable 1 to right
	Rose, p on front, k on back
	Winter white
	Rose
	Flower garden
	Ebony
	Make eyes

TOP FIN, KNIT TWO

• Top Fin is made in two-colour rib. With RS facing, k is in black and p is in purl. Black stitches are cabled to the left or right depending on which side of the fin you are working.
• Cast-on 14 sts in black.
• Row 1. * k1 black, p1 white, rep. from * to end.
• Row 2. *k1 white, p1 black, rep. from * to end (yarns are held on this side).
• Row 3. k1 in black, * Hold 1 white st on cable needle and hold at back of work, k1 black, p st from cable needle in white. Rep from * to last 2 white sts, p2tog.
• Row 4. k white sts, p black sts, to last 2 black sts, p2tog.
• Row 5. rep row 3.
Now form Fin ends
• Twist first 2 sts over bringing white to the back. P2tog in black then p new st 5 times by moving it from one needle to the other. Cut thread and pull it through. You have made one fin end.
• Rep this last procedure 3 more times. Each fin end is one st shorter, so p that st 4 times on the next one, 3 times on the one after.
• Last 3 sts – twist next 2 sts, p3tog in black, p st again, cut thread and pull through.
• Sew in ends.
The other side of fin is the same but sts are cabled the other way. Follow diagram for help. St two sides of fin tog.

FINS NEXT TO GILLS, KNIT TWO

• With black, cast-on 7 sts.
• Work 4 rows in 2 colour rib, k in black, p in white. Form fin ends by twisting first 2 sts over bringing white to the back, k2tog in black, and continue k this st over and over to the right length. Rep to end of the row. Stitch in ends and attach to fish between points B.

INSIDE FLESH LINING

• Knitted in rose, or another fleshy colour. Follow the shape of the body charts, but knit in plain stocking st.

TO MAKE UP

• Stitch tail ends together, and then stitch up the topside of fish right down to the nose, around the mouth and stop at the bottom of gills.
• Stitch top fin on between points A.
• Stitch gill fins on between points B.
• Stitch the topside of the fleshy lining, and insert into fish, Loosely tack in at the head and tail and then neatly stitch along the belly.

Zoë Ashton-Worsnop
HELLO MANGO

Zoë Ashton-Worsnop spins and hand dyes her own yarns using all kinds of wool and fibres. She makes crocheted items such as scarves, hats and flower pins and sells them through her website, Hello Mango. Approaching yarn and crochet from an artistic perspective, each item she produces is unique.

www.hellomango.co.uk

'I come from a rich creative heritage, as both my mother and my grandmother were extremely talented, working on crafts such as crochet, tatting, painting and drawing. Like my mother and my sister, I have synaesthesia, whereby when I hear words and sounds, particularly music, I see colours – a wonderful gift for a fibre artist. I rediscovered my creative side whilst learning how to be a mother to my newly born son. I rediscovered knitting and finally mastered crochet. After a few months of making hats and scarves I realized that you can only wear so many, so I decided to start selling them at craft fairs and over the internet. I started designing items with particular themes and colorways in mind. After a while I began to notice other websites, particularly American crafters like Pluckyfluff and My Paper Crane who were spinning these fantastic yarns and using unusual colours and textures. I realized that I had to learn how to spin my own yarns as I simply could not afford to buy those that they were selling. After a shaky start and several swear words I got the hang of it. I taught myself how to dye the wool before and after spinning so that I could use the colours, and combinations, that I felt inspired to use. After a few months of spindle spinning, I bought a spinning wheel and have never looked back.'

Fairytale Forest Hat

Zoë Ashton-Worsnop

MATERIALS

• Dark Brown DK Chenille (or equivalent brown DK/Worsted weight yarn)
• Handspun Fairytale Forest Yarn: I spun my own yarn but a good alternative is Rowan Biggy Print or a similar weight yarn in brown, dark and light green. Also include a small amount of cassette tape into the yarn for texture. (Approx 55 yards/165 feet.) This is roughly DK/Worsted weight yarn although Handspun is uneven and unpredictable.

ABBREVIATIONS

ch = Chain
dc = Double Crochet
sl st = Slip Stitch
sts = stitches
bpdc = Back Post Double Crochet
fpdc = Front Post Double Crochet

NOTE

This pattern has been written using US notations. The end of each round is turned to keep the back seam straight.

INSTRUCTIONS

• Using Handspun yarn, make a ring using either traditional chain or adjustable ring method.

• Ch2, 12dc into ring, join to 2ch with sl st (12sts).

• Ch2, 2dc in each st around, join to 2ch with sl st (24sts).

• Turn & Ch2, *1dc in next st, 2dc in next st*. Repeat from * to * all way round. Join (36sts).

• Turn & Ch2, *1dc in next 2 sts, 2 dc in next st*. Repeat * to * all way round. Join (48sts).

• Repeat row 4.

• Turn & Ch2, 1dc in each st around. Join.

• Repeat row 6, fasten handspun yarn off.

• Using brown chenille, begin ribbed section.

• Turn & Ch2, 1dc in each st around. Join.

• Turn & Ch2, *bpdc in first st, fpdc in next st*. Repeat * to * around and join.

• Turn & Ch2, *fpdc in first st, bpdc in next st* Repeat * to * around ensuring that each bpdc corresponds with the fpdc on previous row and vice versa. This is to ensure a ribbed affect is achieved.

• 11 – 14, Repeat rows 8 and 9 alternately until desired length is achieved.

• Cast off.

The Church of Craft

A spiritual community that champions a Do-It-Yourself ethic, the Church of Craft promotes the crafty way of life to its congregation. It began informally, in the San Francisco Bay Area in the spring of 2000, as a craft club organized by Tristy Taylor, who wanted a regular place where people could meet while working on all manner of crafts. Meanwhile, in New York, Callie Janoff, an artist becoming fascinated with the potential of craft, had been asked to officiate at the wedding ceremonies of three couples with whom she was friends, and become ordained as a minister in the Universal Life Church. She decided that what she got from crafting was what some might call religious and wanted to form her own version of a Church to celebrate this feeling and share it with others. The Church of Craft was officially born in October 2000, when Johanna Burke brought Taylor and Janoff together. According to Taylor 'the two of us, talking together in Johanna's pink boudoir, hatched the Church of Craft idea, and Callie immediately took me down to the basement and ordained me over the internet. It couldn't have happened the way it did, without both our ideas and thoughts and vision. I really do feel that the "gestation" occurred over our entire lives, in that

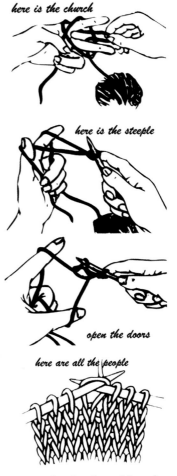

here is the church

here is the steeple

open the doors

here are all the people

we wouldn't be who we are without all the experiences we've had and books we've read and art making we have done. And I think our soul connection with each other and our desire to gather and make a community really helped this idea come together.' The Church of Craft could be seen as a giant piece of art. Performance art of the very best kind, where the people involved don't always know that they are making art. The concept of the Church has been adopted by others and there are Churches of Craft being opened across America and spreading around the world. Friends made within the Church of Craft are meeting and taking their crafting seriously, as they consider the impact of their work and its place in their own sense of spirituality.

Images and design by C. Kelty. Used by permission of the Church of Craft.

Knitted Graffiti

In the summer of 2005, two women in Montrose, Texas, were frustrated with the number of knitted projects that they had started with eager enthusiasm only to soon abandon in dusty corners of their houses. They were passionate about knitting but were, by their own admission, 'not the knitted sweater vest or baby blanket types,' preferring to come up with more adventurous uses for their knitting. They began to think about what they could do with their half-finished projects. Then an idea struck. For what they had planned they needed to go undercover. Calling themselves AKrylik and PolyCotN, they formed Knitta, the most unlikely graffiti tag crew, and began bombing the inner city, armed not with spray cans but with stitched works of art. With their lovingly handcrafted pieces of knitting they covered public monuments and telegraph poles, bikes and abandoned beer bottles. AKrylik explains, 'One of first evenings out was spent wrapping a pole and a tree with what would have been a baby blanket and a child's poncho, had I ever finished them.' Each time they shared their secret about what they were doing more people joined and together they began knitting specially designed pieces, knitting tree huggers, cozies for bikes and door handle covers.

They emerge gleefully under cover of darkness to hang their projects from the fabric of their town. So that people know that they are graffiti tags and not just discarded knitting, they hang a hand off each piece. They imagined how surprised people would be when returning to their parked cars the next morning to find its aerial covered by a multi-colored cozy, admitting, 'It's very exciting to stand around and watch to see what people do when they see a piece. We're often caught mid-installation and have to play the part of a surprised spectator.'

They often receive requests for commissioned pieces, from people who want their property tagged. AKrylik explains, 'A favorite tag was a kid's bicycle in Rice Village. He'd sent a message about the possibility of having his bike tagged. Then another message, complete with a picture of the bike, asking us to PLEASE tag his bicycle. He told me exactly where it would be locked up, on what days and at what times. I couldn't resist. He was very excited about it.'

This is a friendly form of urban graffiti and a new use for knitting. AKrylik explains, 'Graffiti done well can be smile-inducing, both the artistic content and the somewhat rebellious, secretive nature of graffiti in general. We felt that knitting needed to evolve into something a bit more edgy and streetwise, while a more positive and acceptable light could be aimed toward the act of graffiti-ing. We wanted to take both concepts and turn them on their respective heads.' They compare their work to traditional graffiti. 'Personally, I love graffiti art. I'm not a huge fan of basic tagging (with a few exceptions), but I have no problem whatsoever with the awful, prefabricated building next door being beautified in the middle of the night by an incredibly talented individual armed with a can of spray paint. I really don't understand the animosity toward this artform. Did that building look so great beforehand? Was it such an asset to the community? We feel we're tagging your corner stop sign or your car antenna with something bright and positive...something that can be removed, if you so choose, with little to no effort. They're usually buttoned or slipped on, occasionally with a few knots for added longevity. However, these little rays of sunshine are often removed by folks that like them so much, they want them for their very own. The installations don't tend to stay up very long.'

Word soon spread about their knitting activities. 'This was originally an idea that we thought would be funny within our little pocket of Houston. Once the Houston Press article came out, and the responses started pouring in, first on MySpace, then on our web site, we knew we were on to something with exciting potential.' They recently took their activities to New York for a weekend of tagging across three boroughs with approximately sixty pieces.

AKrylik's ambitions for knitted graffiti are big. 'I think it would be amazing to see different "crews" popping up all over the world, installing little knitted hugs across their cities.' Their message? 'Knit and tag away, people of the world. Cover your town in one big blankie! But please make up your own crew name and individual tags. The Knittas are from Houston, Texas. We'd love everyone to start alternative graffiti groups, but I think we should all have our own crews and represent in our own style.' New groups are being formed all over the world: Hell's Knitters on America's West Coast, Seedy Stitch Crew in Virginia, Klickety-Klick in London and The Green Garter in Glasgow.

Craftivism

Craftivism is based on the idea that activism + craft = craftivism. Each time you participate in crafting you are making a difference, whether it's fighting against consumerism or making items for charity. At the forefront of this Craftivism movement is Betsy Greer, who adopted the term, using it for her website, www.craftivism.com (See her project for rugs, pages 193-196). She explains, 'I first starting getting into this idea in late 2002/early 2003, when the bulk of the antiwar protests were going on. While I always wanted to get my voice and opinion heard, I was never quite sure that yelling was the best way to go about it.' Craftivism, as Greer says on her site, is 'the idea that activists can be crafters, and crafters can be activists.'

There are many examples of what Betsy Greer labels 'Craftivism'. The Ottawa Committee of the World March of Women draped Ottawa's Sparks Street in what they called a social safety net. The net, 33.5m by 2.5m was made up of nearly 3,000 colorful knit or crocheted 30cm square patches, sent in from Europe and North America, attached to a large fishing net with twist-ties. The large net, which hung from the lampposts, lined a block of the pedestrian mall. In front of the Canadian Council of Chief Executives, another group of craftivists sang, 'Knit and purl/This is how we change the world/Stitch by stitch/Square by square/Claim the vision/Take the dare.' This concept of craftivism may be growing steadily, but the concept is not new. In 1911, British suffragettes in the Women's Tax Resistance League unveiled a banner depicting Britannia, the goddess who personifies Britain, and the slogan 'No Vote No Tax' in embroidery. The message was both obvious and ironic – the women used a traditional, feminine skill to make a powerful and controversial statement.

Knitting can be used as a protest, the knitting itself can be a petition. The UK-based project, Knit A River, demands water and toilets for everyone through a knitted petition. Made from 15cm by 15cm blue squares, which each take the place of the traditional use of a signature, the petition is a knitted river. The river will travel to all future WaterAid campaigning events to demand access to clean water for 1.1 billion people around the world. (www.wateraid.org.uk)

Lisa Anne Auerbach
STEAL THIS SWEATER

Following the 2004 US presidential election in which John Kerry lost out to George W. Bush, Lisa Anne Auerbach disbanded www.knittersforkerry. com and started www.stealthissweater. com – which refers to Abbie Hoffman's *Steal This Book*, a survival guide for those who fantasize about anarchy. Steal This Sweater combines an anarchic political stance with a love of knitting sweaters. Armed with a knitting machine and a real knack for inventing striking images and slogans Lisa Anne offers a variety of patterns on her site aimed at encouraging everyone to take a leftwing stance and resist the onslaught of consumerism.

www.stealthissweater.com

'There is a craft element to my work, but I don't consider myself a crafter per se. I chose to make sweaters because they are a great medium. I had to learn to knit in order to produce this type of work, and I have learned a lot about knitting traditions, patterning, and cultural history. It is my hope that my work will influence people to take control of their own production and make things that are unique and full of their own ideas.

In terms of why craft is enjoying popularity right now, I can only speculate or speak from my own experience. My mother is an incredible quilter in Illinois. Though I was not interested in learning to quilt when I was a child, I was influenced by her work, which contained strong imagery of our lives and experiences. From her I learned that something handmade can speak volumes about the maker. Though she might disagree, I believe that there is no point spending the time to make anything that ends up looking generic or 'just like the pattern'. In grad school, I worked primarily with photography. After school, I was broke and no longer had access to a darkroom, so I learned to knit and started making sweaters as part of an art practice. It wasn't until years later that I finally got a knitting machine and was really able to make the sweaters I was interested in making.

Currently, I teach photography and am again making photographs. When I teach conventional black and white photography to university students, they are really excited about the process, the chemistry and the cause and effect inherent in photography. For a generation raised with computers, the hands-on processes are a novelty.'

Body Count Mittens

Lisa Anne Auerbach

Body Count Mitten pattern courtesy of *KnitKnit* issue #6, 2005 (www.knitknit.net).

Knitting can start important conversations. You can knit whatever you want, including political messages. Los Angeles artist Lisa Anne Auerbach created the 'Body Count' Mittens as a way to start conversations about the Iraq Invasion. On the first mitten she knitted the total number of American soldiers killed in the conflict. The second mitten again features the total number of American soldiers who had lost their lives by the time she was working on the second mitten. Held next to each other, the two mittens illustrate the increasing number of those killed. Auerbach intends these knitted artifacts to show the personal tragedy of war. You can use the medium to present whatever you want. Search for some increasing figures which are particularly meaningful to you. When people ask you what the numbers mean, you can explain and let others know your views. They are an ideal means of communication. Their ambiguity causes curiosity and this can transmit powerful messages.

MATERIALS

• Two skeins worsted weight yarn (this project used Brown Sheep single ply Lamb's Pride). Choose two colors that will contrast one another.
• A small quantity of worsted weight in a third color for trim (optional).
• One set of double pointed needles, #2.
• Tapestry needle for weaving in ends.

GAUGE

6 stitches/inch (Worsted weight yarn knit with small needles will result in a dense, thick fabric.)

INSTRUCTIONS

Changing Colors
• First of all, do not be intimidated. Switching from one color to another while knitting takes some practice, but it is relatively simple to pick up. One of the simplest methods is to knit with one strand in the Continental style and throw the

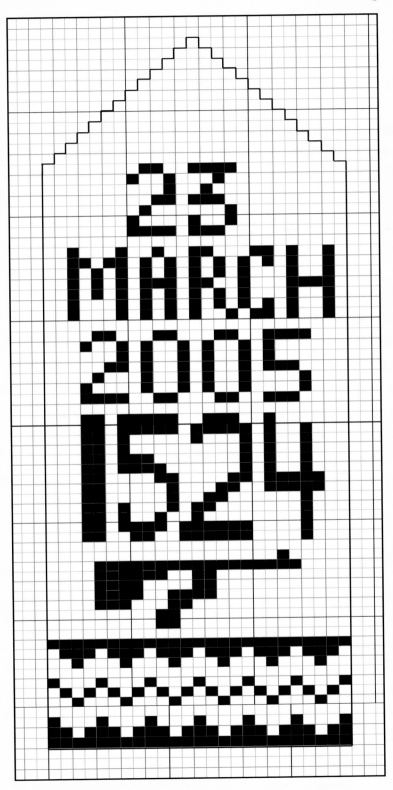

other strand as for American style knitting.

Designing
• The chart in this project shows figures for March 23, 2005. Your dates and numbers will be different, so you will need to design your chart to reflect the current information. For designing the numbers you want to use you will need to plan your pattern on knitter's graph paper. The proportions are different from regular graph paper, reflecting the shape of a knit stitch, which is wider than it is tall. You can buy knitter's graph paper at a knit shop or download it from the internet.

Knitting
• Start by marking off 25 stitches in width. Because of the lack of space on the mittens, you may have to abbreviate the name of the month. Be sure to center the text.
• The object knitted between the cuff and the date is a gun, an AK-47, but you can use whatever icon you wish.
• When knitting from the chart, begin at the bottom. Since these mittens are knit

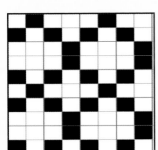

in the round, use markers of some sort to delineate the edges of the pattern area.
Cast-on 54 stitches or make an I-cord of 54 stitches (maybe in a contrasting color) and cast-on from that.
• First round: Purl.
• Second round: Knit.
• Third round: Begin cuff pattern. Choose any cuff pattern of 12 or 13 rows you'd like, design your own, or try the one I used (see illustration, left).

• After the cuff pattern is finished, knit one round plain. Purl one round. Now: 25 stitches are the back of the hand. 25 stitches are the front. And 2 stitches are on either side.
• Divide stitches on three needles. Keep the 25 back stitches together, and split the others evenly.

The Wrist
• To give the decrease knit 2 stitches together on the wrist side, 12 times in the first knit row.
• Knit 6-8 rounds plain, swapping colors if you want stripes.

The Hand
• Increase 5 stitches on the wrist side in the first round.
• Begin patterns. For the palm pattern, use something small and simple. A plain

lice pattern would work fine, or you might choose a small pattern.

• On either side of the 25 stitch back pattern, knit one in the main color and one in the contrasting color, so you'll have foxy stripes up the sides of the mittens.

The Thumb

Mark the 3 stitches on the palm side next to the side stripes. These stitches will be increased from 3 to 11 stitches as follows:

• After three rounds, increase in the first of the 3 stitches and last of the 3 stitches. You will have 5 stitches marked for the thumb.

• After 3 more rounds, increase in the first of the 5 thumb stitches. You will have 7 stitches marked for the thumb.

• Continue in this way until there are 11 stitches between the markers.

At the same time you're working increases for the thumb, continue to knit around in pattern.

• Try on the mitten to figure out where you'd like the thumb to branch out of the palm and when you get to that point, knit the 11 thumb stitches in a contrasting color before continuing on in pattern.

• After the mitten is knit to the top, this yarn will be removed and the 11 stitches will be picked up on dp needles and knit to make the thumb.

• Continue knitting in pattern until the mitten is big enough to begin decreasing. The number of rows will vary based on hand length, gauge, etc. Don't make the mittens too short. It will take about an inch or so to decrease by decreasing 2 stitches on each side of the stripes, so work that into your calculations.

• Finish the ends of the mittens with a tassel or just leave them plain.

• Knit the thumb by cutting the scrap yarn and picking up the 22 stitches.

• Pick up an extra stitch at either side of the thumb opening by twisting the yarn at the corners and making that into a stitch.

• Knit until the thumb is long enough, then begin knitting 2 stitches together every other row to decrease it to a point.

• Weave in the ends.

Radical Craft

In recent years, many textile artists have used knitting as an integral part of their art, blurring the distinction between art and craft. For example, the artist Shane Waltener made a site-specific, web-like piece embedded with a text from the French semiotician Roland Barthes. (According to him knitting has been 'long underrated because it is "women's work"'.) Kirsty Robertson took the binary code from an existing computer virus called Code Red and converted it into a piece of knitting. Rather than rendering the virus harmless, this act was actually a form of re-encoding; one could imagine it being carried invisibly (worn as a garment) until the wearer decided to decode it. Canberra artist Bronwen Sandland utilized over a hundred knitters in her piece 'housecosy' where she covered her entire house with knitted squares.

This shifting division between what is seen as being art and what is seen as craft is fascinating many artists. In 2002, artist Sabrina Gschwandtner founded an artist's publication dedicated to the intersection of traditional craft and contemporary art. She describes the moment she began imagining the magazine into existence. 'Riding my bike home from a park one day in the fall of 2002, I thought, "I'm going to interview Jim Drain and Jamie Peterson, and make a zine about handcraft and conceptual art." As I was riding, pushing down on each pedal, I thought, "knit," "knit," "knit," "knit." "KnitKnit" became the name for my zine, my art project, and my way out of having to choose either knitting or fine art – I could do both.' Others must have been feeling the same as *KnitKnit* is now published twice a year, full of interviews, profiles, articles, reviews and drawings and is sold at bookstores, yarn shops, boutiques and art galleries across the US, Australia, Canada and Europe.

Grant Neufeld
REVOLUTIONARY KNITTING CIRCLE

The Revolutionary Knitting Circle, is a social activist group based in Calgary in Canada, a 'loosely knit circle of revolutionaries', founded by Grant Neufeld. Realizing the potential of knitting as a visible means of protest, a simple, portable means of constructive resistance, he put out a unique call for protest:'Knitters of the world, unite!' The Revolutionary Knitting Circle was born.

www.knitting.activist.ca

'We need as communities to be able to take care of ourselves because when we are not able to take care of ourselves, we end up dependent on others – in this case the corporation – to survive.' This sense of self-reliance is vital as when we rely on others, they can tell us what to do, like eating genetically modified foods or clothing made in child-labor dependent sweatshops. Knitting is used to remind us that we can be responsible for our own lives away from corporate dominance.

In preparation for their protests the group knitted banners, which could also be used as blankets. Neufeld explains, 'What we're doing is symbolic. Another thing about the blankets is that they represent warmth and security because we feel we are losing our security.' This banner should be knitted as a group with each person knitting their own square. When sewn together, the blanket reads 'Peace Knits' and can be used as a banner calling for peace. It is a symbolic way for a group to knit together their collective protest.

Photograph: Revolutionary Knitting Circle

Peace Knits Banner

Grant Neufeld (Revolutionary Knitting Circle)

This pattern describes how to construct a banner from a number of squares so that the work can be divided across a number of knitters.

3	5	3	2	7	5	7	5	3	2	16
2	8	2	9	2	4	2	1	2	9	16
3	1	3	2	3	3	7	6	3	2	16
16	3	7	3	11	3	3	2	7	5	1
16	2	10	2	12	2	1	2	14	15	1
16	3	7	3	13	3	1	3	7	6	1

The Squares

• Each square is 6" (although you can scale it differently depending on how big you want to make your banner.) Use a knit stitch (not stockinette) to get a rib across the square.

• The default pattern has dark letters on a light background. The 'patchwork' style of this pattern means that any combination of colors can be used on each square, so long as there is high contrast between the light and dark (medium range colors should not be used). Many of the squares are identical, hopefully making it easier to divide up the work.

• The squares can be knit, crocheted or stitched together. The result will be best if the seams are tight.

• You need to stitch a border around the whole banner.

• To support a pole to be used for carrying the banner, you can either attach loops, or a long knitted/cloth tube, along the top for the pole to go through. Depending on how you are going to carry or hang the banner, you may also want to add some weight to the bottom corners.

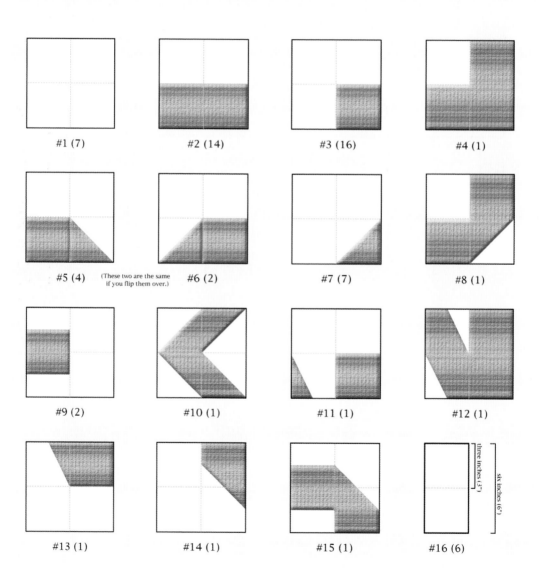

#1 (7)   #2 (14)   #3 (16)   #4 (1)

#5 (4)   (These two are the same if you flip them over.)   #6 (2)   #7 (7)   #8 (1)

#9 (2)   #10 (1)   #11 (1)   #12 (1)

#13 (1)   #14 (1)   #15 (1)   #16 (6)

three inches (3")   six inches (6")

Peace Fleece

More and more crafters are realizing that the simple and meditative act of knitting can be used to express emotive messages, protests and proclamations. Peace Fleece (www.peacefleece.com), a small yarn supplier in Maine, US, has developed a way to promote peace through the production of unique yarns. Committed to the promotion of world peace, they make yarn blended from wool sourced from conflicted countries. The organization began in 1985 when Peter Hagerty and Marty Tracy started to buy wool from the Soviet Union in the hope that through trade they could help diffuse the threat of nuclear war. Since then they have worked with shepherds in Russia, Kyrgyzia, Israel and the West Bank, as well as in Montana, Ohio, Texas and Maine. By working with people who tend livestock every day, they hope to find a common ground that slowly leads to mutual understanding and economic interdependence.

Many of the people Peace Fleece work with overseas are in the midst of political, social or economic crisis, some living through war. The wool trade is essential to their economic and emotional survival. Peace Fleece explains, 'Knitting is a peaceful activity. Sheep are archetypically placid. When they cross a road that you are driving down, there is nothing to do but wait. It never crosses your mind to honk the horn or try to drive around – you just turn off your engine and admire the ungainly woolly lumps brushing past your front bumper. Knitting starts with the sheep.' This attitude has fuelled their trade and Peace Fleece works tirelessly to promote the idea that the peace of knitting can go some way to reducing the World's conflict. This may appear at first to be an impossible ambition but remember that knitting is a meditative activity, both solitary and social, mathematical and artistic, complex and simple – an ideal metaphor for peace.

Brand Sabotage

Artist Cat Mazza is an active member of the new knitting movement, a frequent participant in New York knitting groups and firm advocate of the rise of popularity of knitting. She suggests that the current craft resurgence is due to a combination of factors. 'We depend so much on technology in contemporary society that I think people are finding pleasure in handcrafting. Given that so much of what we use, buy and wear is manufactured in a way that is invisible to most of us, being able to construct something that begins with just needles and yarn is really satisfying.'

Recognizing that knitting can mean much more than just looping wool over sticks, Cat Mazza uses the craft to voice her own protest against unfair working conditions in sweatshops within the textile industry. Today when clothes can be bought so cheaply the work that goes into making them is undervalued and the maker often exploited.

After traveling to urban knitting circles throughout America, she found that most of the knitters she met saw their knitting as a relaxing hobby, a creative pastime, rather than as an alternative to mass consumerism. This inspired her to prompt knitters to make the connection between making things by hand and anti-sweatshop activism. She explains why knitters are the perfect group to lead this anti-sweatshop campaign. 'Knitting can be considered a radical practice in a culture so used to buying things and knit hobbyists are a meaningful group to mobilize on the sweatshop issue because they understand the labor process that goes into making a garment.' The thinking being that once you have knitted a jumper yourself then you will have new respect for the hard work that goes into making one.

Mazza began to realize the potential of knitting as a means of social protest and to draw attention to the issue of corporations using sweatshops she devised a unique means of knitted protest. On her website, www.microrevolt.org, she offers a free online application called KnitPro, which translates any uploaded digital image into a custom knit or crochet pattern. Traditionally making graphics in knitting requires sketching out patterns on a grid. Mazza explains that when working with digital images she realized that the squares were similar to the pixels that make up digital images and that the translation of one pixel to one stitch could be automated.

Knitted 'Nike' blanket: photography Cat Mazza

She encourages people to use this program to engage in what she calls 'logo-knitting' – knitting logos such as the Gap or Nike logo into a garment such as a wristband, jumper or leg warmers. This act of reproducing copyrighted logos is an attempt at brand sabotage. Mazza recognizes that 'the allure of a brand is sold through advertizing whose consumption is triggered through the logo's resonance. Meanwhile, most corporate monopolies capitalizing on this symbol have unfair labor practices. The workers who actually sew the logo into the garment are suffering in sweatshop conditions.' Logoknitting subverts this mode of unfair production. The garments developed using KnitPro and the way in which they are created, are a simple form of knitted protest. By knitting the logos of such well-known sweatshop offenders onto clothing, Mazza hopes to prompt discussion on how advertising, labor, production and consumption are all intertwined. This logo-knitting is an ironic gesture, a symbolic act of resistance that promotes awareness concerning the disregard for the work and skill that goes into making mass-produced clothing.

Although knitting is a simple apolitical act, using a traditional skill for a radical means in contemporary society can be revolutionary. The title of Mazza's MicroRevolt project is loosely based on French philosopher Felix Guattari's concept of 'molecular revolutions', which states that small acts of resistance in everyday life can initiate wider social change. To choose to knit is a simple decision but it is the reasons behind your act that can spark revolutionary ideas.

'Barbie' legwarmers: photography Carrie Dashow

Elizabeth Stottlemyer
HOBBLEDEHOY

Though she has been crafting since the age of nine, Elizabeth Stottlemyer's decision to take this interest one step further – and actually spin and dye the yarn that she uses – is an inspiration to us all. She is keen to remind people that taking pleasure in the basic sensual experience of wool, appreciating the soft texture of an item or choosing the colours it is made in, can be far more gratifying than simply grabbing clothing off a rail as an impulse buy in high street stores, barely noticing what you are purchasing.

www.hobbledehoy.etsy.com

'I first began spinning this Spring with a drop spindle that I ordered from the internet. I quickly became addicted to the comforting plush texture of wool, and spent seven hours straight trying to master the frustrating twirling stick, but did not emerge successful until the following week. I have always enjoyed teaching myself new crafts using guide-books and various internet forum communities such as www.craftster.org, but spinning has been an enormous achievement. Once I became accustomed to the feel of spinning, and after purchasing a second-hand Babe Fiber Starter spinning wheel, I wanted a more direct connection with the fiber. I decided to develop a deeper relationship with the wool by dying it myself. Using a variety of tutorials and tricks from trial-and-error, I developed a simple set of steps in order to dye wool with powdered sugar-free drink mixes. If followed correctly, KoolAid mixes are every bit as lightfast and permanent as professional dyes. However, I would recommend professional acid dyes for very specific colors or large batches of wool where consistency of color is guaranteed. As an alternative to impulse purchases and instant gratification, spinning is a slower process which has taught me how to focus on the simple pleasures of soft wool and rich color combinations. Each skein is a unique individual which can take between four and five hours to complete (from dying to setting).'

KoolAid Dye

Elizabeth Stottlemyer

KoolAid is a fantastic dye for beginners, which works best on animal fibers. I have used KoolAid on alpaca, wool, mohair and angora, and all have absorbed the bright sugary colors marvellously.

MATERIALS

- Wool roving or top (this is the undyed natural fibre)
- Gloves
- Pots
- Food coloring
- Vinegar
- KoolAid (www.koolaid.com)

INSTRUCTIONS

Preparing the Wool

• Fill a pot 2/3 full of warm water, and add several tablespoons of vinegar. Pre-soak the wool for 20 minutes. This helps to even out the wool's porosity, which will create more consistent colors.

On the Stove

• While you're anxiously waiting to add color to your soaking lump of wool, get busy on the stove by filling a pot 2/3 full of water. Set to 'Medium Heat'. Add two tablespoons of vinegar, and two or three packs of KoolAid. The more KoolAid you use, the more intense the color will turn out. The wool will dye much lighter than the color of the liquid, so keep that in mind too. To alter KoolAid colors, or add more variety, use drops of food coloring.

Back to the Wool

• Gently squeeze excess water out of the wool, and submerge it into the pot of dye. While the wool is in the dye-pot, be careful not to agitate it too much, or it will felt, making it very difficult to spin. Also, it is best if the wool does not simmer. I have found that the bubbling contributes to felting. While the wool is soaking up the dye, you can sprinkle more KoolAid powder onto the wool to create interesting color effects, or drop/squirt/splash food coloring into the wool as well. The wool will soak up most (if not all) of the color, and you will be left with a pot of clear water and dyed wool.

• Allow the wool to cool down before rinsing it out, and always rinse with a temperature similar to that of the wool. Be careful not to shock the wool with cold or cool water, as it will felt it. Once the wool has been rinsed, hang it outside (in a bird-free zone) to dry in the sun. If the sun is stubborn, hang the wool in your shower.

Photography Elizabeth Stottlemyer

244

CRAFTY IDEAS

Unknit Your Sweater

Wool is expensive but there are ways around this problem. In charity shops and thrift stores you can buy good quality wool in the form of woolly jumpers. Then all you have to do is unravel them and you have plenty of wool for reusing. It is a brilliantly simple idea and means that an ugly sweater can have a new life as a cute handknitted garment. Not only is it thrifty, it is also helping the environment. Recycling existing clothing into something new without using new resources is something we could all be doing. So, let's start unknitting.

Choosing Your Sweater

• Look for the best quality wool you can find. It doesn't matter at all about the style of jumper – it's just the wool you want. If the jumper is bobbled or felted or made from poor quality wool or synthetic material then it won't produce good quality wool.

• Avoid sweaters with serged seams. This is where the pieces of the sweater were cut and sewn together so the yarn is not a long continuous strand. This is something to avoid, as if you unravel one, you will end up with hundreds of very short strands. Look at the inside seams and examine the end stitches where the pieces are sewn together. If the end stitches have not been cut and look intact then you'll be fine. If you gently pull apart the end stitches you should be able to see the strand of yarn that was used to seam them together. Serged seams are fairly obvious, look for overstitching (usually done in sewing thread) and cut end stitches.

Unknitting

• The first step to reclaiming the wool is to undo the seams. Snip carefully with scissors or you will cut through the knitting. If this does occur, don't despair; you will just have lots of smaller balls of wool.

• To unravel, be sure to start at the end where the garment was cast off not cast-on. If you begin where the knitting was cast-on, where the wool is looped over stitches, you will end up with a tangled mess.

• You will need to something to unwind the wool onto, producing skeins. You can use someone else's hands, held about a foot apart, or the back of a straight back chair. Keep unwinding until you come to the end of a length of wool. Join to the next piece of wool with a loose knot and keep unraveling. It may take a while to unravel the whole garment but it will be satisfying as you see your skeins of wool grow.

Soaking the Wool

• Next, you will need to clean the wool so that it is ready to use again. Soak the skeins for a couple of hours in hot tap water and a little handwash soap or shampoo. When the water is cool rinse well in more clean, cool water and gently squeeze out water. Take sure that you don't wring the wool as this will affect its shape and it may start to felt. Next, drip-dry over the bathtub on plastic coat hangers.

• When it is dry, the wool will probably be crinkley, fixed in the shape of the previous knitting. Once it has dried, winding it into balls will help to straighten the wool. Make sure that you wind gently so that you don't stretch the wool out of shape.

Animal Free Knitting

For those who do not want to use animal by-products in their knitting there are plenty of alternatives, rapidly becoming more easily available. You can choose from yarns made from: synthetic yarns (acrylic, nylon, polyester), cotton, bamboo, soysilk, hemp, banana silk, linen or flax.

Knitted Experiments

Whoever told you that you could only knit from wool? Certainly not me. You can experiment using different materials. With some materials you might just make a knotty mess but then with the next you try you may get some fantastic results. You shouldn't be afraid of using unusual materials – the more unexpected the better. To get started, you could try knitting with: string, paper, plastic, wire, ribbon, video or cassette tape.

How To Start Your Own Knitting Group

Pauline (KnitChicks)

TIPS FOR KNITTING IN PUBLIC

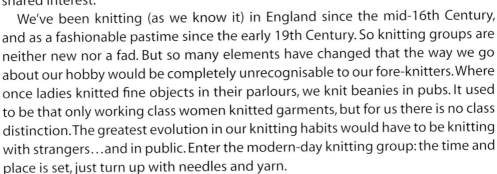

The first time at a knitting group can be like going on a blind date: 'Will I recognise them?', 'Will we get along?', 'What if it's no fun?' The anxiety may be the same, but the result is not. The beautiful simplicity of the knitting group is that everyone has a shared interest.

We've been knitting (as we know it) in England since the mid-16th Century, and as a fashionable pastime since the early 19th Century. So knitting groups are neither new nor a fad. But so many elements have changed that the way we go about our hobby would be completely unrecognisable to our fore-knitters. Where once ladies knitted fine objects in their parlours, we knit beanies in pubs. It used to be that only working class women knitted garments, but for us there is no class distinction. The greatest evolution in our knitting habits would have to be knitting with strangers…and in public. Enter the modern-day knitting group: the time and place is set, just turn up with needles and yarn.

Knitting groups can be very informal, without leaders or rules. Finding groups that are suitable for you is as easy as logging onto the internet. The hardest part is finding the courage to just turn up…like the blind date! Unlike the date, knitters always have something to talk about: current projects, new products, patterns, magazines, all the paraphernalia that makes up our hobby. But what to do if there is no suitable knitting group nearby? Organize one yourself – it's really not that hard. The key ingredients are choosing an appropriate venue, getting the timing right and spreading the word.

VENUE

For me, the deal-breaker is adequate lighting. There is no point trying to seriously knit if you can't see what you're doing. It helps to meet in a smoke-free place. No-one, not even the hard-core smoker, wants to give (or receive) a gift that smells like it is anything but brand new and not like you picked it up off the pub floor. Imagine knitting baby booties that smell like an ashtray before they're even finished. Finally, refreshments are vital. Knitting groups are sociable – enjoy a cup of tea or a glass of wine with the group and relax.

TIMING

If you're starting up a group from scratch, choose a time and date that suits you. After all, at least you know you will be there. But consider the demographic, who are the knitters most likely to turn up? If it's a work-type group obviously 3pm is out of the question, ditto for mothers of school-age kids. Obviously you can't cater for everyone's schedules (hence look after yourself first) but do try think about where people might travel from/to and factor that timing in.

SPREADING THE WORD

You've got the time and the place, all you need now is for others to know about it and come. The internet is the best resource of all. Message boards, knitting/craft sites and blogs are the best places to find out all sorts of information. But don't forget those not online. Community centres, local newspapers, schools, universities and guilds are always interested in helping people getting busy and crafting. Once again, consider your demographic when posting these notices.

When the big day arrives, do some preparation. Bring some spare needles and yarn and a few patterns. Make sure your own project is not complicated (or at least at an easy part) so you can concentrate on chatting this first time. Have your latest knitting magazine, anything that might kick-start a conversation if people are feeling shy.

Most importantly, make everyone feel welcome. Despite the name, knitting groups are not just for knitters – you'll encounter all sorts of crafters who are looking for a bit of socialising and inspiration.

Knit Online

The internet is a huge part of the rising popularity of craft – as a means of mass communication it is the ideal tool for bringing crafters together. Craft forums, such as www.craftster.org and www.getcrafty.com work as virtual sewing circles where people show their finished projects and share patterns and designs. Have you ever wondered what to do with those free and unwanted AOL CDs that come through your letterbox or an unusual piece of furniture you found in a skip? If you have, then this is the place you should go. There are craft swaps where people who have never met make and send unique hand-crafted gifts to each other and get a similarly handmade gift in return. They often take the form of a crafty challenge – requiring that you make something for a kitsch kitchen or rework a vintage pattern. There are bloggers who document their love of all things crafty, attracting thousands of devoted readers daily. There are crafty podcasts where people share various crafting techniques and discuss the growing rise of craft. There are online shops where people are selling their crafty wares. It is all about communication, people wanting to share their crafting with others.

On January 14, 2006, knit blogger Stephanie Pearl-McPhee, otherwise known as Yarn Harlot, challenged knitters to join her in the 2006 Knitting Olympics. To participate, a knitter would cast-on a project during the opening ceremonies of the 2006 Winter Olympics in Torino, and have finished it by the time the Olympic flame was extinguished. By the first day of the Olympics, almost four thousand knitters had signed up for the challenge. The sudden popularity of this event illustrates just how many crafters are at work, communicating online, eager to get working on their next project and excited to take part.

PAPER
AND
INK

People have always used the medium of paper and ink to express themselves, from circulating their views in printed form to screen printing their own T-shirts. Printing can be rebellious, it is an uncensored act. Putting your words and pictures into print is a way to express your ideas, to a greater extent than is possible with your voice alone. When I first started to self-publish my own words in the form of zines, I realized the potential of printing, the power of paper and ink. Today's crafters have realized this too – printing their own words and pictures on paper, and even making their own books and stationery.

You can never ever have too many notebooks. I have dozens, of all different sizes, paper types and colors. Some for writing down study notes, serious thoughts, books to read, ideas, 'to do' lists. I have them in my bag, on my desk, on my shelves. Actually I am probably rarely more than a few metres away from a handy notebook. It's even better if you make them yourself. A couple of years ago I went to a notebook making workshop at the Independent Publishing Resource Center in Portland, Oregon and learnt how to turn old hardback books into notebooks. It is a perfect use for old books you might have with an appealing front cover but know you are not interested in reading. You carefully gut the book, cutting out all the pages and then sew blank pages in their place. It makes a brilliant notebook, functional and quirky too. It has been a great use for all the old hardback books and annuals that I have bought in junk shops just because I like the cover, or I admit because it had a funny title.

This kind of simple bookbinding is a great skill to learn. You can make covers for anything, from collections of photos to stories you have written. You can finish a project off with a handmade cover or just make another valuable notebook.

Themba Lewis
MT PLEASANT PRESS

Mt Pleasant Press is a loosely co-operative design and printing company working out of a damp basement in the Pacific Northwest that utilizes cumbersome, out-dated, tedious technologies to make small run print propaganda and unique handmade designs. Letterpress, stencil, block print and screen-print techniques are used to create posters, record sleeves, shirts, patches, broadsides and all sorts of other things. The shop uses soy-based inks, primarily dumped and donated papers, and is chemical and toxin free.

'Everybody is creative. Creation is liberating and expressive. I have never considered myself a crafter or an artist, but I'm stubborn about getting things done that I start, and I start things all the time. It makes me anxious if I don't have a project in the works.

Growing up in Washington DC, I was attracted to the cultural currents that challenged the dominant features of life surrounded by government, power-brokers and massive institutions. Groups like Food Not Bombs seemed so much more effective at getting things done and Riot Grrl was starting to be a term that people recognized. Shows were fabulous places to find zines and flyers and music and other creations that seemed to be so relevant to how I wanted to live my life. It was inspirational. I guess if there was a time when I first encountered and engaged in the "crafter culture", that would be it. Shortly thereafter I was trying to design posters and tape covers in my room. I spent loads of time at copy shops laying things out and manipulating photocopies.'

Take it to the Streets
THE ART OF SPRAY-PAINT STENCILLING

Themba Lewis

As a craft, spray paint stencilling – and the ability to create multiple finished products – has worked its way into posters, T-shirts, record art, zine covers and art prints, each, by the handmade nature of the result, simultaneously common and individually unique. The extension of punk, do-it-yourself ethics is undeniable in the art of stencilling; after all, the stencil is one of the cheapest and most accessible art forms in existence. It requires only a razor, spray paint and a cereal box, and anybody can do it. Much like screen-printing, letterpress and offset printing, stencilling is a process of layering colored images on top of one another in order to create a finished product. This is done through the cutting out of patterns in sturdy templates and producing images by setting those templates against a surface and spray-painting them, thus creating an image defined by what areas of the template spray-paint could pass through and what areas it could not. It is a process of layering for complexity, based in simple images, that can be either extremely quick and straightforward, or perplexing and complicated depending on the intended outcome. This means you have to plan ahead and take things one step at a time. If you haven't stencilled before, I would recommend starting with a one-color or two-color image just to get on your feet; to learn what it's like to choose an image that will transfer well to the medium, to cut the templates, to register layers, and to paint it.

CHOOSING AN IMAGE

Stencilling is not the most careful work and unless you are meticulous in your technique, details can easily get lost or become a mess. High contrast, blocky, bold images therefore tend to work best. Keep in mind that the finished product is made up of layers of color – solid blue on top of solid red for example – and complexity and depth come out of that process, so keeping each individual layer simple may be to your advantage. At the same time, too many layers can complicate things and lead to frustration, so keeping the number of colors down can also be helpful. Stencilling is one of those art forms in which simplicity not only looks better, but is critical to the process. Of course, hand-drawn images work great, but it's also possible with the help of a photocopier or computer to make high-contrast black and white 'negatives' from pre-existing images, like photos. Ultimately you will need to have separate images for each template ('color separations'). What this means is that if your end result is a three-color picture, you will need to construct your image in three parts, each to be placed on top of the previous, in layers. This process can be done in different ways and whatever works best for you is best. Use your imagination – some helpful ideas could including tracing, drawing your image in steps (layer by layer) or using a computer to separate an image into color layers.

MAKING THE TEMPLATES

Which material to choose for the template depends on how many prints you intend to make and how long you want the template to last. Papers tend to absorb spray paint and warp the more times you use them, so sturdier templates (like opened, flattened, cereal boxes or cardboard) hold up over longer usage. Thinner templates, like cardstock or file folders, work just as well and are easier to cut, but may not survive through as many runs. Make sure that your image is at least a few inches smaller than your template. That way, when you are at the spray-paint stage, you won't have spillover spray outlining your template.

There are two good ways to get your image onto the template. The first is to draw it on directly, the second is to draw or print it on a separate piece of paper and use a glue stick or spray adhesive to attach the paper tightly to the template. This second method has a few advantages. Firstly, it allows you to use photocopies or printouts. This can come in handy if you have separated your colors through Photoshop or something like that and can print each layer out on a separate sheet of paper. The second is that if you are making the image by hand you can draw it first on a piece of paper in its entirety and then use subsequent pieces of paper to trace the segments of the drawing that are to be different colors, thereby creating color separations, each on its own sheet of paper! Each of these pieces of paper can then be glued to separate templates and you're ready to start cutting.

CUTTING THE TEMPLATES

Make sure you have a clear space, a sharp razor and good light. Also be careful that you are working on a surface that can get marked up, because the razor will certainly cut into your tabletop, work desk, or whatever you happen to be using. Lay your first template out in front of you. At this point the image should either be drawn directly on it or glued tightly to the top of it. It should also only represent one of the colors of the finished product. X-acto (razor) knives can be bought at almost any art supply store and are shaped like a pen, which makes them easy to use. Start tracing around your image with the razor, careful that the blade is going all the way through the template. Keep in mind that any piece you cut out of the template is a place where the spray paint will go through and onto the surface you'll ultimately be stencilling on when it comes to the spray-painting stage.

At this point, once you've cut your templates, you're ready to try it out. There are a few tricks to this, particularly in making sure that each layer lines up with the previous (this is called correct registration) and that the layers are done in the correct sequential order so that a base color, like for example a background, doesn't accidentally cover a foreground detail color.

PLANNING YOUR LAYERS

Planning your layers is an important step to consider even before cutting your templates, however when it is time to do the spray-painting you ought to make sure that you know which layers go over which and in what order they need to be painted. This isn't so complicated for a one or two color stencil, but once it gets to three or four colors this can get confusing. The 'bottom' layers (most often the background colors) should be sprayed first, then more detailed layers.

GETTING CORRECT REGISTRATION

The easiest way to register layers correctly on top of one another is just to eyeball it and not really care too much about precision. This method is quick and may be quite effective, but unless you're looking for intentionally loose results, it can be frustrating. With a careful eye, the results can be really close, but some of the following ideas might help for more consistent results. The best method is the placement of special registration guides within the image itself. I generally use dots, one on each of the four corners of my template. Cut the dots out of the template when you cut the image out and make sure to cut dots out of each subsequent template so that if the dots are in alignment when the templates are placed on top of one another, the registration is right. Then, when the first stencil is spray painted, dots appear at the corners of the image. When the first spray has dried, and it's time for the next template, simply align the dots on the second template with the dots sprayed into the corners of the image and registration should be close to perfect.

STENCILLING

This is the fun part. Once you've designed your image, made your templates, and planned your spray-painting order, you're ready to go. Make sure you are in a space with good ventilation and be aware that spray paint may end up on the things around you. Place your first template over whatever surface you plan to stencil. (This can really be just about anything, as spray-paint adheres to all manners of

surfaces – I've been in houses with stencilled refrigerators and I've been gifted stencilled towels.) Make sure the stencil is flat against the surface. The flatter the template is, the clearer the lines you'll end up with – if the template is raised up off the surface, spray paint can find its way under the template and either smear or create fuzzy areas. One trick to keeping the template flat against the surface is to weigh it down with coins or other small objects. This may become more necessary as you make multiple copies and the template starts to expand or warp by soaking up spray paint. Holding the spray paint can at least six to eight inches above the stencil template, and keeping your hand moving (so as to create even paint distribution), start spraying. Too much paint increases smudging and drying time, so don't feel like you need to drench your image. Once you're sure you've painted all the parts of the template that need to be painted, slowly lift the template from the surface, using both hands on opposite corners (peel the template off the surface, in other words). This process can be delicate, particularly because the template itself can smudge the fresh paint if it slips. Repeat the process for each subsequent layer, being careful to let each previous paint job dry before doing the next. Laying a template down on wet paint can lead to disaster, as the template can stick to the drying paint and ruin the image and the template.

Stencil art is public art. Rarely are stencils 'one-off' pieces. Stencilling can be incorporated into all sorts of other art designs to create great texture and sometimes unpredictable results. A stencilled paper may be subsequently photocopied, or photocopied on to, for instance, or silk-screened, or even letterpressed. Layers can be manipulated in any manner of ways and colors can be manipulated. It's an experimental medium, so have fun with it. Make your own media.

Kate Bingaman
OBSESSIVE CONSUMPTION

Like many of us, Kate Bingaman has a love/hate relationship with money, shopping, branding, credit cards, celebrity, advertising and marketing. Noticing her growing obsession with consumer culture, she decided to document all of her purchases. The website she created in 2002 was produced not only to document her purchases, but also because she decided to create a brand out of the process, to package and promote. She is currently hand drawing all of her credit card statements until they are paid off and also spends her time consuming, documenting and making.

www.obsessiveconsumption.com

'My mother and father were professional weavers during the late 1970s through the early 1990s. I grew up going to art shows with them during the summers and really absorbing the industry of making whether I wanted to or not. I never intended to be an artist. I was dead set on becoming a broadcast journalist my first couple of years of college and then I took a graphic design class and my mind was blown. I worked as a graphic designer after college for a few years and kept on thinking that I needed to be doing more and that I needed to be making work for myself and so I entered graduate school. I received my MFA in 2004 and during those three years my work focused and I stopped thinking of myself as someone who only wanted to produce graphic design work, but as someone who just always wanted to make great work no matter what media I had to use. Crafting just happens to be another means to a way. I do a lot of work on the computer and I love that, but my favorite working times are when I am sewing pillows with my mother or using my Gocco in my studio or assembling zines. The hand work is incredible satisfying.

For me my interest in craft fits in with my search for the real. Society is so consumed with shopping, celebrity and the mass-produced that satisfaction is gained from MAKING objects with your own two hands.'

Go Gocco!

Kate Bingaman

The Gocco is a little blue screenprinting machine with a devoted cult following. Popular in Japan since its invention in the 1970s as a way for families to produce their own greetings cards, it has been embraced by the contemporary crafting community worldwide as a quick and easy screenprinting machine.

Despite its growing popularity outside Japan, the Gocco is being discontinued by its maker Riso. www.savegocco.com has been launched to try and save the quirky little machine. Unlike screenprinting there is no emulsion involved, but like screenprinting you burn an image into your screen and can print multiples of one image easily over and over again. Like a stamp, you press the image onto the paper. One thing about the Gocco that I really enjoy is that you can use it to print on all types of surfaces: I have printed on folders, wood, sticker labels, CD labels, paper bags, T-shirts and regular old paper.

This tutorial is a general overview that will make the Gocco a little less intimidating. Many things (good and bad) I have learned were through mistakes. I have noticed with many Gocco users that some techniques work well for some users and some do not. Please do not hold me accountable if something doesn't go correctly. Some of my tips will work for you and some you will develop on your own. Using the Gocco and making it work for you is largely dependent on experimenting and exploring.

MATERIALS

• A Gocco machine. The more accessible one is the Gocco PG-B6. They are still plentiful on Ebay and supplies can be found in several places (see resource list).
• Paper or card
• Inks

INSTRUCTIONS

Creating your image

You may either draw your image with the carbon ink pen (one is provided with the Gocco machine) or draw your image and scan and print it from your printer or photocopy it. Black and white laser printers work because they use toner, laser copiers do not work because they use a different type of toner that is carbonless. The Gocco bulbs react to the carbon to burn an image. Make sure your image is carbon based or it will not work. If drawing is not your thing, scan in clip art or other images that you find appealing. Get creative! Remember to keep your image under 4x6, though I have made multiple screens and printed images much larger than 4x6. Again, get adventurous. The Gocco can do a lot if you approach it with no fear! I am going to be printing some

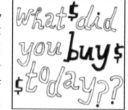

hand-drawn type for the cover of a zine. I scanned in the type, cleaned it up in Photoshop, scaled it to 4x6 and then printed it using my HP 1012 black and white laser printer.

Place Artwork

• The Gocco has a gridded, sticky foam pad, but after many uses it loses its stickiness and gets dirty. I have taped a piece of cardstock to the gridded, sticky foam pad. I noticed that when I was using the pad that the grid would transfer onto my screen when I exposed an image. I didn't like that at all. Placing a piece of cardstock over the pad eliminates the grid from transferring.

Exposing the Image

• Gocco bulbs come in packs of ten. Two are needed to expose each screen and they are not reusable. They are basically old-fashioned flash bulbs. Sometimes inserting the bulbs is a bit tricky. Make sure to push and twist when placing the bulbs. If they are not placed correctly they will not flash off. I have placed one bulb correctly and one incorrectly and it winds up only exposing half of the screen. If this happens

to you allow yourself to be frustrated for a moment, because it is frustrating, but carry on and be aware of the need for correct twisting and pushing.

• Once bulbs are correctly placed into the hood, the hood needs to be placed into the main machine structure. Make sure the arrow on the hood is matched up with the arrow on the main machine. The silver reacting points should be facing towards you. These two parts, if matched up correctly, will fit tightly together.

• This is the fun part. Now that all parts are in place, take both hands and press down. HARD. This will set off the bulbs and your screen will be burned! Expect a quick flash of light.

• Raise the hood and your artwork will be sticking to the screen. Keep it there. Do not peel off.

• Remove the screen.

Inking the Image

• Time for the ink. I still haven't removed the laser print because I like to ink the screen with the paper backing still attached. Keeping the paper attached helps me apply ink to the screen and it also doesn't let the ink leak out of the screen onto the table. If you do remove the paper, no big deal, just place something behind the screen while you apply ink so that it doesn't get onto your surface.

• The Gocco ink has the same texture and consistency as cake frosting. Make sure you cover the area well.

• I am choosing to use two colors for this print. There are many ways to include multiple colors in your prints. If your image is more detailed you may make separations and burn multiple screens with each screen filled with a different color of ink. You may also buy foam ink blocking material and block many areas on one screen and fill each with a different color of ink. Or you may choose to forgo the ink block material and let your colors mesh together like I am doing.

• After you have applied your ink, pull the plastic down over your ink and pat the plastic with your finger to flatten out your ink. Make sure that the ink covers the burned image.

Printing

• Remove paper artwork from the screen.

• Place the screen back into machine with mesh screen facing towards you. You now have the following layers (from top to bottom): plexiglass top, plastic film from top of screen, ink, exposed screen, printing paper, cardstock bottom (if you choose to use it) and grey foam pad.

• Place the material that you want to print on onto pad.

• There are many methods of registering the image. I have pretty easy registration with this particular piece because it just needs to hit anywhere on the pink surface. With more detailed placement I print on scrap paper and take note of where the image falls. I either mark on the white cardstock where I should place my paper each time so it prints in the same place or I take the cardstock off and use the sticky, gridded foam pad and count the square grids and mark with masking tape where the paper should lie. Finding perfect registration is something that comes through trial and error. Again, don't be afraid to experiment.

• Once paper is placed, bring the top of the Gocco down and with even pressure, press the top down onto the paper. Hold for a second or two and then lift up.

• The paper will stick to the ink. Peel paper off and you have a print. Keep printing! I have printed editions of five hundred before with only having to re-ink the screen a few times.

• To re-ink the screen, simply remove screen, peel back plastic and reload the spots where the ink has been used up.

• It takes a few hours for a print to dry completely. Evenly place your prints out for drying. Once you have finished printing, clean your screen and store for reuse. To clean your screen, take a plastic palette knife or spatula and scrape off extra ink. Place ink in a small square of tinfoil and wrap for later re-usage. Make sure that you place a piece of newspaper underneath the screen as you are cleaning. I also like to reinforce my screens with clear packing tape. It strengthens the cardboard frame and lends itself for multiple uses. Towel off extra reside and ink. Allow your screen to dry and then wrap the screen in wax paper and store. This will be very awkward when you first try to clean your screens. Keep with it. The process will become easier and less messy. I promise.

Resource list:
www.dickblick.com   www.thinkink.net
www.welshproducts.com   www.goccoshop.com

what$did
you buy$
$today?
buy$
Independence Day
Richard Ford
JOHN STEINBECK
STEINBECK
STEINBECK
STEINBECK

Sugene Yang
ALL THIS IS MINE

Sugene Yang claims her inspirations as mail, zines, libraries, tea and ephemera and through her website All This is Mine she sells her beautifully crafted handmade goodies. All This is Mine started as a zine of the same name, but over the years it has grown to encompass Sugene's other creative endeavors. Bags, shirts, notecards, bookplates, stationery, stickers and journals, are all examples of things which may be included. Everything is made in a limited edition.

www.allthisismine.com

'I always loved arts and crafts. As a child I spent a great deal of time drawing, cutting and pasting, making all sorts of things, and reading.

In college I became a Fine Arts major, and I focused on making art that was thoughtful, had a point of view, and allowed me to express myself in an effective way. It was intense and therapeutic, but I also craved an outlet to make stuff that was simple, casual, self-indulgent, and fairly meaningless. I was also attracted to art movements that celebrated the ordinary and everyday. Fluxus became one of my favorite movements to read about, and I also grew enamored of mail art and zines. My own philosophy of art was that it was and should be inclusive and that everyone had the capability to be an artist.

After college I still had the need to create, but I was so exhausted from my day job, that most of what I made then was just for the sake of making something. My love for anti-art kept me making zines and cheap multiples, and my desire to create something out of nothing drove me to learn new skills and crafts. All This is Mine has grown to include everything that falls under this premise of making whatever I feel like making. It's cheap, straightforward and simple. It's not about hidden meanings; it's just creation and craft and immediate gratification.'

Coptic Bound Sketchbook

Sugene Yang

MATERIALS

- A variety of different papers for covers, end papers and text pages
- Four dull point needles (tapestry needles or bookbinding needles work well)
- PVA glue and brush
- Board for covers
- Ribbon (optional)
- Awl
- Heavy thread
- Envelopes (optional)

INSTRUCTIONS

When making a book, start from the inside and work your way out. That means that you should make your text block first (the paper inside the book), then use that to measure the size of your covers. After you've cut your covers, cut the paper/fabric you will use to decorate them. This will ensure that everything works out, size-wise.

Choosing your paper

This is the part that makes your book special – the paper inside. The project shown here includes high quality, thick drawing paper in different shades and a section of watercolor paper. You can use any paper you like, such as graph paper, engineer paper, sheet music, comic book pages, etc. You may also choose to include envelopes within a book to hold ephemera and scraps and to create a different look.

Testing Paper Grain

Now it is time to talk about grain, which is a basic rule when it comes to bookbinding. Paper, cardboard, fabric – they all have a grain. You probably noticed the grain in things like paper or napkins when you were a kid and trying to rip things neatly. Here's an easy way to illustrate the concept: Take a piece of paper. Rip it one way. Then rip it the other way. Was one rip easier and cleaner than the other? (The answer should be yes.) The cleaner rip is with the grain, and the messier rip is against the grain. You don't have to rip everything though. The preferable way to test grain is to give your stuff a little bend. Roll up a few inches and bounce it a little, then do the other side. For things like book board, you can just flex it a little one way and then the other to see what direction flexes better. This all comes into play because the number one rule in bookbinding is this: the grain for everything needs to go from top to bottom (not side to side!). This is so the page lays open nice and flat and relaxed when you open the book. (P.S. Now that you know the rule of grain, you can break it if you want.)

MAKING SIGNATURES

• Gather all the papers you'll use in the text block. If needed, cut your papers to the size you want, remembering that each sheet will be folded in half for the book.

• Now it is time to make signatures. A signature is a group of folded papers. To make a signature, fold about five sheets of paper in half, one-by-one.

• Then nest them together. The signatures will be neater and tighter when you fold the papers individually than if you stacked them all together and folded it as one big thing. That is your first signature!

• Sewing the signatures together is what this project is all about, so make a few more signatures. For my book, I used five signatures. Pile all your signatures together and admire them as the heft of the book.

MAKING THE COVERS

• Now that you have your text block, you can use it to measure the covers. In Coptic bound books, the height of the covers is exactly the same as the height of the text block so that the book doesn't sag when it's standing on a shelf. After all, there's no spine but just a little bit of string holding it all together. This is more important for bigger, thicker books.

• Cut two covers out of binder's board. This can be davy board, cardboard or mat board or what-have-you. It is helpful to have fancy equipment like board shears (board shears look like a giant paper cutter) for this part, but you can make do with several passes of a sharp blade and a straight edge.

• You may want to use the covers as they are, especially if you are using an interesting material like wood or metal. But the traditional route is to cover these with paper and/or cloth. If you use cloth, be careful of glue seepage. The book in this project uses some pretty wrapping paper and a German Dresden bird.

• To cover the board, cut the paper about 1-1.5" around the cover. Trace the outline of the cover on the back of the paper with a light pencil line.

HOW TO DO A GOOD GLUE JOB

• Place a sheet of newsprint under the thing you are gluing.
• Always brush outwards, off the paper onto the newsprint. Do this on all sides.
• Then lift your project and fold the newsprint in half (gluey sides together). Keep doing this to keep your workspace clean and not to get glue on undesirable parts of your book.

• Spread PVA glue on the back with a brush within the pencil line. It's okay if you go out of the lines a little. Glue your cover down.

• Turn it over and burnish it and make sure the surface is nice and smooth.

• Snip the corners of the papers close to the corners of the board. The paper should be about 1/8" from the corner of the board. Then brush glue on the little paper flaps around the board.

• Fold up the flaps around the board.

• If you want to add a ribbon to tie your book closed, now is the time. Cut the ribbon 2" longer than you need. Glue these 2" to the inside of the covers. Make sure that the ribbon is adhered to the cover all the way up to the fore-edge.

• Cut the endpapers – the smaller paper that will cover the seams. This is the inside cover of the book. You can use plain paper that will complement the other parts of your book. This project uses sheet music cut down to size. The endpapers should be about half an inch smaller than your covers. Brush PVA onto the back of the endpaper (see 'how to do a good glue job') and glue it on. Don't forget that you have a front and back cover. Make both of them!

PREPARING FOR BINDING

• Fold a piece of scrap paper that is the same height as your book. Mark your sewing stations. This should be an even number, and if you're just starting out you may want to start with just two. It's good to have sewing stations near the ends of the book as this is what will give the book support. Now this scrap will be your template for making holes in your signatures and covers.

• Place the template in the middle of a signature and use your awl to make a small hole. Hold the signature at a 90 degree angle, and put the awl in at a 45 degree angle so that the holes is right on the crease. Do this for all the signatures. For the covers, you want to have the same spacing, but put the holes around 1/8" in from the edge.

BINDING THE BOOK

• A thicker thread will show up the pretty braid at the side. The book pictured used four holes/four needles. You will, however, need to have a needle for each hole. In these instructions, two holes means two needles. Because they are sewn in pairs, there must be an even number of holes.

• Cut a piece of heavy thread (can be bookbinding or embroidery thread about the span of two arms length. Thread each end with a dull point needle (tapestry needles, or bookbinding needles if you have them).

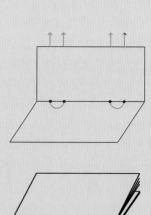

• Take the first signature and sew each needle through a hole from the inside. (If you have more than two holes, then pair up the holes adjacent to each other. You will do the same thing to each pair of holes.)

• Take the cover and line it up next to the signature. Take your needle and enter the cover from the outside. Pull the needle through the hole to the inside of the cover (between the cover and the signature), and to the outside of the stitch. Tighten those stitches.

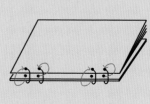

• Go back into the first signature from the outside to the inside. Once inside the signature, cross over your needles. This means that the needle that came out on top will go back down the bottom, and vice versa.

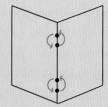

• Now both your needles are hanging outside the book. Pick up the second signature and enter the holes from the outside to inside. Inside the signature, crossover and exit to the outside.

• Count back two signatures and sew around the stitch. Just stick your needles between the cover and the first signature and between the two rows of stitches. Sew back out around the stitch by pulling the needles to the outside of the stitches. No crossover or anything tricky here. Tighten that sucker. You can decide if you want to loop from the inside out, or you if you want to loop from the outside in. Whatever you do, just do it the same way all the way through.

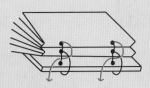

• Pick up your third signature and enter from the outside in. Once inside, crossover and exit to the outside of the book. Count back two signatures (this time you're sewing between the first and second signatures) and loop again the same way you did before. This part is the refrain. Now you can just keep adding signatures this way until you run out of signatures. Don't forget to tighten your stitches.

• Add all the signatures until you are ready for the back cover. Enter both of your needles from the outside of the cover, and have them exit on the side of the stitch you've been doing. Count back two signatures and loop around the stitches as normal. Go back into the last signature from the outside. Once all your needles are inside the signature, tie the ends together and cut off the tails.

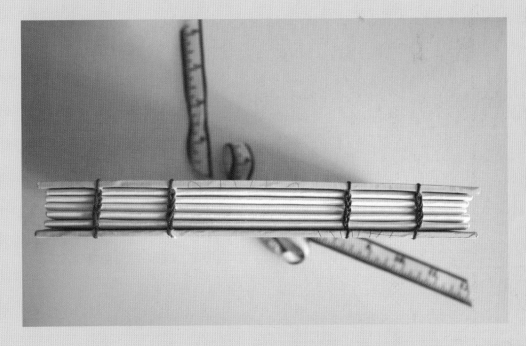

Jill Bliss
BLISSEN

Jill Bliss specializes in working with other independent artists and businesses to create useful, functional items from reused materials in limited editions.

www.blissen.com

'My crafty resourcefulness is a result of a childhood spent in the suburbs of the San Francisco Bay Area and a rural farm in Northern California, with parents who both made and made-do with whatever materials were at hand. My father is a life-long tinkerer. He built our farmhouse, farm equipment, my childhood toys and bikes, and even his own computer from a kit back in the 1970s. Every fall, I assisted my mother, who made and sold crafts during the Christmas season to supplement the family income.

My adult life has been filled with the usual low-pay jobs that go hand in hand with many years of art school training, necessitating the need for crafty resourcefulness in my daily life.

The limited edition goods from recycled materials I make for www.blissen.com usually stem from a need that I or a friend have. Can't find the perfect wallet to fit in my front pocket? Well, I'll just make it then. Once I've perfected it for myself I'll make more of them for my shop and others. Each new material or wish list a friend gives me is a new, unique, fun challenge. The designer in me sees a problem to be solved.'

Paper Pad Cozy

Jill Bliss

MATERIALS

- One pad of paper (any size you choose)
- Fabric

INSTRUCTIONS

Cutting Your Pieces

- Measure the pad of paper you'd like to use. Double the width, and add the height of the paper pad plus half an inch. This is the width of the outside of your cozy. The height will be the height of your paper pad plus half an inch.

- Add another inch to this height and width, to allow for ½" seam allowances on all sides. Measure this square on a piece of paper and cut out. This will be your outside and lining pattern piece.

- Using your outside pattern piece as your guide, create a shorter piece for the pencil/pad pocket, as well as a small front pocket. For both pocket patterns remember to add 3/4" to fold over the top seam.

- For the outside pattern piece cut one outside piece of fabric, and one lining piece of fabric. Cut one piece of fusible interfacing for the outside fabric as well. Both pockets need one piece of fabric each.

Making the Cozy

- Iron the interfacing on the back side of the outside piece. Iron the 3/4" fold-over for the top of both pockets.

- Topstitch both pocket fold-overs.

- Topstitch 1" wide pencil pockets on the pencil pocket, with the lining piece behind it.

- Place the small front pocket on top of the pencil pocket and lining. Place the outside fabric, face down, on top of all the pockets. Sew ½" away from the edge on both sides and the top.

• Turn inside-out with the small pocket and outside on one side, and the pencil pocket and lining on the other. Sew bottom edge.

• Turn the small pocket inside-out so that it is on the inside of the cozy. Fold the cozy in half as you would to close it, and crease by hand or iron. Using the center crease as your guide, topstitch the center.

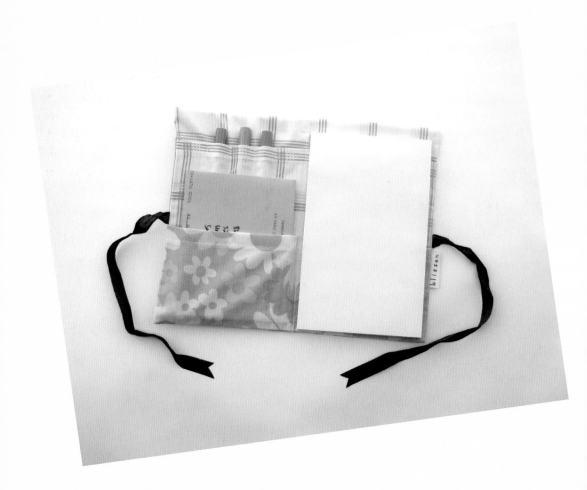

Rebecca Craig

Keen to promote the reuse of unwanted items, Rebecca Craig makes jewellery out of packaging and recycled materials as well as small toys and other objects she finds lying around. Her materials range from the most unlikely – for example, darts flights – to the more traditional – papier maché from old newspapers. She takes a simple delight in transforming the old into something new.

'I used to draw endlessly when I was a kid – amazing landscapes as well as books about people who were flower blossoms who'd discover secret treasure – with such an imagination it was no surprise when I ended up doing a degree in fine art... I was a bit taken aback though when college knocked all my delight of art right out of me. By the time I graduated I just wanted to make cool things that needed no endless justification so I started making jewelry from lego heads...and it didn't stop there.

I think that craft is popular right now because you can create amazing stuff and people actually want to buy it! And if they don't want to buy it you can wear/use it yourself – or give it to friends at Christmas. More seriously, I think people are generally starting to get a bit sick of all the mass-produced accessories that shops chuck out. They are starting to develop a taste for one-off interesting, vibrant objects and items that only small scale crafters can offer them.'

Papier Maché Bangle

Rebecca Craig

MATERIALS

- 1 strip of cardboard
- Flour/wallpaper paste or PVA glue
- Newspaper
- Images from a magazine
- Yacht varnish

INSTRUCTIONS

- Firstly cut a strip of cardboard and curve it round your wrist so that it falls off easily. (It should be wide enough to fall off to allow room for the papier maché.)

- Prepare a papier maché paste (you can use 1 parts flour to 2 parts water, or wallpaper paste, or PVA glue mixed with water) and tear up some strips of newspaper.

- Dunk the newspaper in the paste and wrap it around the cardboard template lengthways. Continue doing this until your bangle is the thickness you desire. You can also scrunch up a piece of newspaper and wrap that around the bangle horizontally to bulk up the bangle a bit.

- Allow the newspaper layer to dry overnight. Once dry cut up some pieces of brightly coloured magazine that will be the outside layer of your bangle. Glue these on with PVA glue so that the bangle becomes hard and shiny.

- Additionally once the decorative layer is on you can varnish with yacht varnish to make the bangle really hard and shiny.

Packing Tape Transfers

To make incredible cheap and easy transfers all you need is a piece of clear packing tape.

MATERIALS

• Clear packing tape
• Magazine images
• A sponge
• Water

INSTRUCTIONS

• Find an image you like from a magazine.

• Carefully place packing tape over the image.

• Use the sponge to make sure the tape is completely stuck to the paper.

• Wet the backside of the paper; you can either dip the whole thing in water, or use a brush, cloth, or just your finger to apply the water. Wait a few minutes for the water to saturate the paper.

• Use your finger to gently rub the paper away; the ink from the image adheres to the tape, and then your image will be left.

Paper Maker

MATERIALS

• Waste paper. Coloured or white, most paper types can be used, but high-quality papers produce better results
• Kitchen blender
• Measuring-jug
• Frame (instructions below)
• Rectangular washing-up basin
• Wooden spoon
• Good quality blotting paper (Or you could use a non-woven fabric such as lint-free domestic cleaning cloth)
• Washing-up sponge
• A heavy weight (some heavy books will do)

INSTRUCTIONS

Making the Frame

The frame is the most important element of the paper-making process. It can be easily bought in craft shops, or made at home and can be reused.

To make it you will need:

• 8 lengths of 3/4" thick wood
• Screws
• Waterproof glue
• Mesh (such as net curtains)
• A stapler and staples

• Cut eight lengths of wood to the size you want your paper to be.

• Join the corners together (making two separate frames) with waterproof glue.

• Secure joints with screws to prevent them falling apart while the glue sets.

• Take one of the frames and choose one face to be the back and one to be the front. Along the back of one of the side members, use the staples to fix the mesh.

• Wrap it around the outside edge of the frame, across the front of the frame, around the outside of the opposite edge, pull it tight and staple it to the back of the opposite side member. Do the same at the top and bottom of the frame, carefully folding the corners, so that the front face of the frame is covered with a taut piece of mesh.

• Leave to dry.

Making the Paper

• Tear your chosen paper into postage-stamp-sized pieces, remembering to remove any staples, glued edges, paper clips and sticky tape.

• Soak paper in a little water to soften it to a pulp.

• Fill the blender with enough clean water for the quantity of paper you're using. The pulp shouldn't be too thick or too watery, so add the water carefully, and adjust as necessary. The pulp should be the consistency of thick wallpaper paste. Avoid making a smooth pulp, as this means the paper could be weak.

• Switch off the blender and leave to one side.

• Fill the basin with clean water, approximately four parts water to one part pulp.

• Pour pulp into the washing-up basin, making sure that the basin has one of its widest sides closest to you.

• Stir pulp with the wooden spoon in order to distribute the particles evenly throughout the water, before pulling your first sheet of paper. Hold the frames firmly together, with the mold mesh side up and the deckle on top creating a frame. The depression is where your sheet will be created.

• Lower the frame into the near side of the basin and gently push it away from you, gradually submerging it until it lies flat under the surface of the water. You may want to move it back and forth to ensure that you get enough pulp on the mesh.

• Holding the mold flat and level, carefully lift it from the basin. But before all the water drains away, gently rock it back and forth. This will help the fibres to mesh together, ensuring that the paper will be strong. Rest the mold and deckle on the basin for about 20 to 30 seconds to allow some of the water to drain away.

• Place a damp cloth on a flat hard surface.

• Remove the top frame. This will leave the paper on the mesh and make it easily detachable.

• Hold the bottom frame almost vertically to one side of the cloth and in one smooth movement roll the mold down so that the pulp is pressed to the cloth.

• Using the sponge, press quite hard on the back of the mesh to transfer the pulp to the cloth. You should be able to see it coming away from the mesh, and reverse the rolling action to lift off the empty mold.

• At this point you can add dried flowers, leaves, glitter, silk threads to create your unique paper.

• Gently press another cloth onto the paper to help with the drying process. Then place the weight of a pile of heavy books onto the paper, so that it dries flat. Leave for 30 minutes.

• Remove the books and the top cloth, and leave to dry in a warm dry place such as in an airing cupboard.

• Once dry, carefully peel each sheet from the cloth and you have your own paper.

Conversion Tables

VOLUME

1 cup = 240 milliliters
1 tablespoon = 15 milliliters
1 teaspoon = 5 milliliters
1 quart = 1 liter

WEIGHT

1 ounce = 28 grams

LENGTH

1 inch = 2.54 centimeters = 25.4 millimeters
1 foot = 12 inches = 30.48 centimeters

KNITTING NEEDLES SIZE GUIDE

Metric (mm)	3	4	5	6	7	8	9	10	12
UK	11	8	6	4	2	0	00	000	-
US	-	6	8	10	-	11	13	15	17

CROCHET HOOKS SIZE GUIDE

Metric (mm)	2	2.25	2.5	2.75	3	3.75	4	4.5	5	5.5	6	6.5	7	8	9	10
UK	14	13	12	-	11	-	8	7	6	5	4	3	2	0	00	000
US	-	B/1	-	C/2	-	F/5	G/6	7	H/8	I/9	J/10	K10.5	-	L/11	M/13	N/15

Further Resources

In Print

Craft

Beal, Susan, *Super Crafty: Over 75 Amazing How-To Projects* (Sasquatch Books, 2005)

Der Ananian, Greg, *Bazaar Bizarre: Not Your Granny's Crafts* (Viking Studio, 2005)

Farry, Eithne, *Yeah, I Made it Myself: DIY Fashion for the Not Very Domestic Goddess* (Weidenfeld & Nicolson, 2006)

Hart, Jenny, *Sublime Stitching: Hundreds of Hip Embroidery Patterns and How-To* (Chronicle Books, 2006)

Kramer, Leah, *Craftster Guide to Nifty, Thrifty and Kitschy Crafts: Fifty Fabulous Projects from the Fifties and Sixties* (Ten Speed Press, 2006)

Linden Ivarsson, Anna-Stina, *Second-Time Cool: The Art of Chopping Up a Sweater* (Annick Press, 2005)

Jackson, Julie, *Subversive Cross Stitch* (Chronicle Books, 2006)

Meyrich, Elissa, *Rip It!: How to Deconstruct and Reconstruct the Clothes of Your Dreams* (Fireside Books, 2006)

Mullin, Wendy, *Sew U: The Built by Wendy Guide to Making Your Own Wardrobe* (Bulfinch, 2006)

Nicolay, Megan, *Generation T: 101 Ways to Transform a T-shirt* (Workman Publishing, 2006)

Rannels, Melissa and Melissa Alvarado and Hope Meng, *Sew Subversive: Down and Dirty DIY for the Fabulous Fashionista* (Taunton, 2006)

Schmidt, Denyse, *Denyse Schmidt Quilts: 30 Colourful Quilt and Patchwork Projects* (Chronicle Books, 2005)

Vitkus Stewart, Jessica, *Alternacrafts: 20+ Hi-style Lo-budget Projects to Make* (Tabori & Chang, 2006)

Knitting and Crochet

Albright, Barbara, *Odd Ball Knitting: Creative Ideas for Leftover Yarn* (Clarkson N Potter Publishers, 2005)

Bliss, Debbie, *Home: 26 Knitted Designs for Living* (Ebury Press, 2005)

Carson, Tsia, *Craftivity: 40 Projects for the Maverick Crafter* (HarperCollins, 2006)

Christiansen, Betty, *Knitting for Peace: Make the World a Better Place One Stitch at a Time* (Stewart, Tabori & Chang, 2006)

Durham, Teva, *Loop-d-Loop: More Than 40 Novel Knitting Projects* (Stewart, Tabori & Chang, 2005)

Gardiner, Kay, Mason Dixon, *Knitting: The Curious Knitters' Guide* (Crown Publications, 2006)

Hardings, Sally, *Quick Crochet Huge Hooks* (Mitchell Beazley, 2005)

Fast Knits Fat Needles (Mitchell Beazley, 2005)

Hargreaves, Kim, *Vintage Style: 30 Knitting Designs from Rowan* (Rowan Yarns, 2004)

Jensen, Candi, *Crochet Bags!* (Storey Books, 2005)

Crochet Scarves! (Storey Books, 2005)

King, Emma, *Fun and Funky Knitting: 30 Great Designs for an Exciting New Look* (Collins & Brown, 2006)

Knight, Erika, *New Knits: 20 Knitting Projects with a Contemporary Twist* (Quadrille, 2004)

Matthews, Rachael, *Knitorama : 25 Great and Glam Things to Knit* (M Q Publications, 2005)

Hookorama : 25 Fabulous Things to Crochet (M Q Publications, 2006)

Mischer, Suzan, *Greetings from Knit Cafe, Stewart* (Tabori & Chang, 2006)

Pearl-McPhee, Stephanie, *Yarn Harlot: The Secret Life of a Knitter* (Andrews McMeel Publishing, 2005)

Knitting Rules! (Storey Books, 2006)

Radford, Leigh, *One Skein* (Interweave Press, 2006)

AlterKnits (Stewart, Tabori & Chang, 2005)

Singer, Amy R, *Knit Wit: 30 Easy and Hip Projects* (HarperResource, 2004)

Stoller, Debbie, *Stitch 'n Bitch Handbook: Instructions, Patterns and Advice of a New Generation of Knitters* (Workman Publishing, 2003)

Stitch 'n Bitch Nation (Workman Publishing, 2005)

Stitch 'n Bitch: A Knitter's Design Journal (Workman Publishing, 2005)

Stitch 'n Bitch Crochet: The Happy Hooker (Workman Publishing, 2006)

Swartz, Judith L, *Hip to Knit: 18 Contemporary Project for Today's Knitter* (Interweave Press Inc, 2002)

Zilboorg, Anna, *Knitting for Anarchists* (Unicorn Books for Craftsmen Inc, 2002)

Craft Theory

Dormer, Peter, *The Culture of Craft: Status and Future* (Manchester University Press, 1997)

Macdonald, Anne, *No Idle Hands: The Social History of American Knitting* (Ballantine Books, 1988)

Rowley, Sue, *Craft and Contemporary Theory* (Allen & Unwin, 1998)

Parker, Rozsika, *Subversive Stitch: Embroidery and the Making of the Feminine* (Women's Press Ltd, 1996)

Online

Craft Magazines

www.adornmag.com — The crafty girls guide to embellishing life
www.craftzine.com — Craft gets a modern makeover
www.helloindie.us — The ezine of the DIY craft scene
www.knitknit.net — Blurs the line between art and craft
www.knitty.com — Online magazine with free patterns
www.magknits.com — Friendly knitting magazine
www.readymademag.com — Magazine for people who like to make stuff

Craft Community

www.castoff.info — Cast off knitting group for boys and girls
www.churchofcraft.org — Worldwide quirky craft community
www.craftster.org — No tea cozies without irony
www.craftrevolution.com — Restoring the appreciation of crafts
www.craftyplanet.com — Saving the world one stitch at a time
www.departmentofcraft.com — Secret agents promoting all things crafty
www.getcrafty.com — Craft forum and blog site
www.knitchicks.co.uk — Find local knit groups in the UK
www.knitting.activist.ca — Revolutionary knitting circle
www.pdxsupercrafty.com — Saving the world from mass production
www.supernaturale.com — Dedicated to DIY crafts

Craft Blogs

www.angrychicken.typepad.com — Documenting beautiful craft projects
www.areathriftyone.blogspot.com — Using re-purposed, thrifted and new materials
www.camillaengman.com — Beautiful art and crafts
www.craftivism.com — Craft and activism
www.craftlog.org — Super crafty blog
www.extremecraft.blogspot.com — Art as craft, craft as art
www.hackaday.com — Electronic modification projects
www.modish.typepad.com — Standing up for the independent crafter
www.notmartha.org — Not Martha, but fantastic
www.myhouseiscuterthanyours.
    blogspot.com — Domestic undertakings with a retro twist

www.paperforest.blogspot.com	Paper art news and ideas
www.redefiningcraft.com	Thinking about craft theory
www.thimble.ca	Arts and crafts blog and shop
www.weewonderfuls.typepad.com	Documenting lovely sewing projects
www.whipup.net	Handcraft in a hectic world

Craft Casts

www.cast-on.com	A podcast for knitters
www.craftborg.com	Two craftoholics share their passions
www.craftychicapodcast.blogspot.com	Hosted by craft writer Kathy Cano Murillo
www.craftypod.wordpress.com	Bi-weekly podcast all about making stuff
www.craftsanity.com	Using craft to tackle the stresses of life
www.driventoquilt.com	The podcast for today's quilter
www.grandmassewingcabinet.libsyn.com	A podcast about fashion sewing
www.knitcast.com	A podcast all about knitting
www.stitch-cast.com	How to sew

Knitting and Crochet

www.bhkc.co.uk	British Hand Knitting Confederation
www.chicknits.com	Modern designs for modern knitters
www.crochetlab.com	Compendium of crochet related stuff
www.tkga.com	The Knitting Guild Association
www.knitting-and-crochet-guild.org.uk	The Knitting and Crochet Guild
www.knitgrrl.com	Fantastic craft books
www.knittinghelp.com	Plenty of knitting help
www.knotjustknitting.com	Freeform knitting and crochet
www.learntoknit.com	Learn to knit
www.menknit.net	Men knit too
www.stealthissweater.com	Stop making scarves. Start making trouble
www.yesterknits.com	Collection of vintage knitting patterns

Craft Supplies

www.hellomango.co.uk	Beautiful bright yarns
www.helloyarn.com	Fine yarn and spinning supplies
www.loop.gb.com	Gorgeous yarns and supplies
www.reprodepot.com	Huge source of reproduction fabric

Craft Kits

www.craftylikeafox.ca	Unique craft kits
www.madewithsweetlove.com	Naughty latch hook kits
www.stickywicketcrafts.com	Bringing you original craft kits
www.sublimestitching.com	Charming kitsch, vintage style embroidery
www.subversivecrossstitch.com	Subversive cross stitch kits
www.threadymade.co.uk	Hot cross stitches
www.woolandhoop.com	Crewel embroidery kits

Shop Crafty

www.31cornlane.com	The Sperber sisters make fantastic bags
www.allthisismine.com	Handcrafted goods
www.birdinaskirt.com	Lovely stationery
www.blissen.com	Collective making super cute stuff
www.boygirlparty.com	Cute art illustrations and handmade crafts
www.bugbrand.co.uk	DIY audio devices
www.buyolympia.com	Shop for Olympia-made goodies
www.copacetique.com	Boutique of handmade goods
www.circlecircledotdot.com	Handmade cuteness
www.cutxpaste.com	Selling a range of crafters' creations
www.dsquilts.com	Home of Denyse Schmidt's beautiful quilts
www.etsy.com	Where indie crafters sell their wares
www.exlibrisanonymous.com	Blank journals made from old book covers
www.gerberadesigns.com	Accessories designed to plant a smile
www.gudonya.com	Bath and body products
www.handmadebyalys.com	Selling illustrator Alys Paterson's work
www.handmadepretties.com	Felt pretties
www.homeofthesampler.com	Order a secret sample package of crafts
www.ibuydiy.com	Links to indie businesses
www.indiefinds.com	Co-op increasing awareness of indie shops
www.karissacove.com	Cute purses galore
www.laurafallulah.com	Unique handbag designs
www.lekkner.com	Custom T-shirt reconstruction
www.lizziesweet.com	Bath and body for the nice and naughty
www.mymy.girlswirl.net	Showcasing independent crafters
www.mypapercrane.com	Adorable handmade plush foods
www.obsessiveconsumption.com	Selling thought-provoking media and crafts
www.ohmystars.net	Tutorials for refashioning T-shirts

www.oyinhandmade.com	Handmade hair and body stuff
www.plainmabel.com	Vintage and artisan crafts
www.primrosedesign.com	One-of-a-kind handcraft items
www.redlipstick.net	Knitting patterns
www.seamripper.net	Sewn items and more
www.sewdarncute.com	Cute sewn items and other crafts
www.sewdorky.com	Makers of fine felted donuts
www.sidepony.com	Hand-printed and crafted notecards
www.thesmallobject.com	Art and craft with quirky designs
www.superfantastico.com	Pins, bags, T-shirts and paper goods
www.supermaggie.com	Handmade crafts
www.susanstars.com	Sewing jewelry, kits, trinkets and gifts
www.thesmallobject.com	Quirky arts and crafts
www.timberhandmade.com	Cute handmades
www.zuzupop.com	Handmade vintage-inspired clothes

Charity Crafting

www.dogshome.org	Knit blankets for Battersea Dogs' Home
www.afghansforafghans.org	Sending handknits to Afghanistan
www.craftersforcritters.com	Indie crafters raising money for animals
www.projectlinus.org	Knitting blankets for children in need
www.warmwoolies.org	Knit clothing for poverty-stricken children
www.wateraid.org.uk	Knit a river

Craft Classes

www.craftgym.com	San Francisco craft studio space
www.makeworkshop.com	New York city craft classes
www.stitchlounge.com	San Francisco craft classes

Craft Fairs

www.bazaarbizarre.org	Not your granny's craft fair
www.craftinoutlaws.com	Alternative craft fair in Columbus, Ohio
www.nocoastcraft.com	Minneapolis craft fair
www.renegadecraft.com	The first indie craft fair
www.urbancraftuprising.com	Seattle alternative urban craft fair